The Pennsylvania
Heritage Cookbook

The Pennsylvania Heritage Cookbook

A Cook's Tour of Keystone Cultures, Customs, and Celebrations

Kyle Nagurny

STACKPOLE
BOOKS

Published by
STACKPOLE BOOKS
5067 Ritter Road
Mechanicsburg, PA 17055

Printed in the United States of America

10 9 8 7 6 5 4 3 2 1

First edition

Cover illustration by Margaret C. Brandt

Library of Congress Cataloging-in-Publication Data

Nagurny, Kyle.
    The Pennsylvania heritage cookbook : a cook's tour of keystone cultures, customs, and celebrations / Kyle Nagurny.
       p.   cm.
    Includes index.
    ISBN 0-8117-2496-4 (alk. paper)
    1. Cookery—Pennsylvania. 2. Cookery—International. 3. Pennsylvania—Social life and customs. I. Title.
TX715.N187   1998
641.59748—dc21   97-32175
                                                        CIP

Dedicated to Mike, Kelly, and Michael,
my wonderful family,
who tolerated a dirty house
and excessive amounts of takeout food
during the completion of this book.

In memory of Grandpop Nagurny and his furry friend, Barney.

Contents

Introduction

Pennsylvania is a place rich in cultural tradition and strong in its food heritage. In researching this book, I found more historical ethnicity, especially regarding food, than I ever imagined possible. This made for a substantial book about the food customs and celebrations of the various ethnic groups that live in the commonwealth.

Pennsylvania is a big place, and in spite of modern technology, I found it impossible to cover every culture, ethnic organization, and related event held in the state. And even if I tried to cover all possible bases, I'd be working on this project twenty-four hours a day and well beyond my life expectancy. (And there are some other things I need to do, like raise the kids and change the litter box.)

I look forward to going back to the many Pennsylvania events and renewing friendships made in the course of my background research. I traveled many miles and hope the book will help motivate you to do the same. There's a lot of culture to explore in the Keystone State.

I plan to use the ethnic recipes on the following pages on a regular basis—for everyday meals as well as on holidays and other special occasions. The recipes are deliciously diverse and most are easy to make. You'll notice that recipe ingredients and methods representing one culture are often similar to those in recipes for another ethnic group. In my judgment, the entire world, not just the United States, is a huge "melting pot" of food customs and cuisine.

Be adventurous. Try some of the recipes that are least familiar to you. Travel to events that seem the most exotic, and by all means, use *The Pennsylvania Heritage Cookbook* to broaden your cultural horizons while having a really good time.

Native America

A Feast in the Valleys

I wish William Penn were alive today to describe in colorful detail his friendly relationship with Pennsylvania's Indians. Although most colonists viewed the Indians as uneducated heathens, Penn grew to know them as a highly moral people with a strong sense of family, values, and higher purpose.

As a result of his good rapport with the Indians, Penn became one of the state's foremost tribal authorities and negotiators, purchasing their Pennsylvania lands under fair and peaceable terms during the late 1600s and early 1700s. Surely Penn must have eaten the Indians' food and known their cooking techniques as well.

Some of Pennsylvania's earliest Indian nations included the Susquehannocks and Delawares (or Leni-Lenape), but the Six Nations of the Iroquois eventually overpowered these groups and took control of their lands. Shawnee, Nanticoke, and Mohicans also existed, but only under the authority of the more powerful Iroquois and their famous Seneca leader and spokesman, Chief Cornplanter.

Like all tribes across the nation, Pennsylvania's Indians lived off the land. Animals, fruits, plants, and grains were the sources of clothing, shelter, and weapons. Fresh streams and rivers like the Susquehanna provided fish, drink, and transportation to tribes like the Susquehannock, for whom the river was named. In turn, the Indian respected the earth and broad waterways for what they gave to him.

Pennsylvania's Indians hunted deer, wild turkey, and bear and plied the streams and rivers for trout, shad, and mussels. They enjoyed wild berries, nuts, and vegetables and grew corn, squash, and beans. The Iroquois held strawberry, maple, and green corn festivals each year, in addition to planting and harvesting celebrations.

While the Indian men hunted and fished, the women kept the home fires burning, cultivated the fields, and prepared the food. They created cooking utensils from animal bones, used wooden mortars and pestles to grind corn and wheat into flour, and cooked in clay pots. Meats were rotisseried over hot stones and served on wooden platters with wooden knives and spoons.

Indians often gathered to feast on just one or two large meals a day, but the women were sure to keep a pot of stew simmering over an open fire for guests or a hungry child seeking a late-night snack. Recipes were simple but satisfying, and meals nutritionally balanced.

The Delaware Indian women, in particular, were considered excellent cooks, and their carefully and thoughtfully prepared meals impressed even the Europeans. They developed delicious recipes using the three "sisters"—squash, corn, and beans—considered the staple foods among tribes. The squash was usually a variety of pumpkin, and other foods such as fish, poultry, insects, potatoes, wild peas, and nuts were combined with the "sisters" in various recipes. The women were proficient at tapping maple syrup from trees and picked wild berries to make preserves.

Corn was considered "the essence of life" and remains one of the most important ingredients in the Native American diet today. Several varieties—blue, red, yellow, white, and speckled—are still used. Blue corn, in particular, has gained some mainstream appeal and is probably the favorite among Native American cooks. Traditionally, corn was boiled, roasted, pounded, ground, and kneaded with flour to create stews, side dishes, bread, meal, dumplings, and even drinks. So that they would have sufficient food during the harsh Pennsylvania winters, the Indians would dry corn just after the harvest and stock enough to last through two winters (in case of extensive crop failures). The women would hang fresh corn on the cob outside for several weeks to dry, sometimes enhancing the process by baking the cobs first. Corn then became a treasured, year-round commodity that was easily rehydrated and used in recipes for hominy, dumplings, casseroles, hot cakes, and breads.

A FEAST FOR THE DEAD

Pennsylvania's Delaware Indians grieved deeply with the death of their loved ones and openly expressed their emotion during the burial ceremony, known as the "mourning over the corpse." The Delawares believed that the body had two souls—one in the blood and another in the heart. As an integral part of the funeral, food was placed on the grave and a meal served to the mourners for eleven days after the burial.

The gravesite food was designed to nourish the deceased with "spirit essence" and on the twelfth day, allow the soul in the heart to rise peacefully to the spirit world. The soul in the blood remained on earth and became a ghost which haunted those who did not provide a feast for the dead.

Valley Spoon Bread

3 cups milk, divided
1 cup yellow cornmeal
2 tablespoons butter

1 teaspoon salt
1 teaspoon baking powder
3 eggs, separated

In medium saucepan, combine 2 cups of milk with the cornmeal. Cook over medium heat, stirring constantly, until mixture is very thick and pulls away from side of pan. Remove from heat. Add remaining 1 cup milk, butter, salt, and baking powder, stirring until blended and butter melts. In medium bowl, beat egg yolks with wire whisk or fork. Add about 1 cup of the hot cornmeal mixture. Return the egg yolk mixture to remaining mixture in saucepan, blending well. Beat egg whites until stiff but not dry. Fold into egg yolk mixture. Spoon into lightly greased 2-quart casserole dish. Bake at 325 degrees for 45 to 50 minutes, or until sharp knife inserted near center comes out clean. Serve warm with butter. Makes 6 servings.

Corn Pone

1½ cups yellow or
     white cornmeal
1½ teaspoons baking soda
½ teaspoon salt

1¼ cups water
1 tablespoon safflower oil
1 to 4 tablespoons
     additional water

In large bowl, combine cornmeal, baking soda, and salt. Make well in center. Add water and oil. Stir just until dry ingredients are moistened, adding 1 to 4 tablespoons additional water as needed to form thick but not stiff batter. Heat griddle until cold water sizzles when dropped onto surface. Lightly brush griddle with shortening. Drop generous tablespoonfuls of batter onto hot griddle. Cook until bottoms are lightly browned. Turn and continue cooking until other side is lightly browned. Serve warm. Makes about 1 dozen.

Forksville, Pennsylvania, isn't exactly on the way to most places, but the journey down scenic, lesser-known roads makes for an interesting trip. The main attraction is the Eastern Delaware Nations' traditional Native American Pow-Wow held in mid-June at the Sullivan County Fairgrounds. This is a three-day weekend of Native American dancing, music, crafts, and storytelling. Like other events of its kind, the pow-wow is effectively designed to raise awareness about Native American culture. Kids, in particular, can learn while they have fun, and they won't even need to crack a social studies book to do so.

Lloyd and Audrey Brandt are Mohawks who own and operate the Mohawk Soup Kitchen. For about fifteen years now, they have driven a mobile version of their Canadian-based restaurant to various pow-wows up and down the East Coast. The Brandts and just a handful of other food vendors have cornered the market on authentic Native American cookery at many of these events, and they took some time out between the lunch and dinner crowds at the Forksville Pow-Wow to talk about their recipes and food preparation.

Contemporary pow-wow food is prepared from scratch and incorporates traditional preparation techniques with more modern methods and ingredients for the sake of convenience. For example, a popular Native American baked good called frybread, made from a simple flour dough, was originally fried in hot lard, but nowadays vegetable oil is used.

Some Native American historians say that frybread evolved from the white man's donations of lard and white flour to the Indian nations during the establishment of reservations across the country. The resourceful Indian women created wonderful uses for such donated ingredients, and frybread was one result. Others say that frybread was created by the Navajos and the bread's popularity spread from tribe to tribe over time.

At the Forksville Pow-Wow, the Brandts made spicy Indian tacos using frybread instead of tortillas as the base. They topped their own homemade frybread with olive oil, cheese, seasonings, and rice or beans plus various combinations of lettuce, onions, tomatoes, and peppers. Seems Indian tacos are a favorite at most pow-wows and other Native American gatherings.

The Brandts also make a delicious buffalo stew from an original family recipe. They cook buffalo meat (supplied by a Minnesota-based butcher) with turnips, celery, carrots, onions, and potatoes and season it all with a secret spice. The stew is then served over wild rice, harvested from lakes in the Keewatin region of Canada. This rice is also used in place of meat to make a delicious vegetarian chili.

For a pow-wow breakfast you might consider a ham and egg scon. Mohawk scons are whole-wheat biscuits that also serve very nicely as buns for the restaurant's buffalo burgers. Other food items at the pow-wow are buffalo chili and Indian corn soup.

The Sullivan County Pow-Wow is held in mid-June on Friday and Saturday from 10 A.M. to 8:30 P.M. and Sunday from 10 A.M. to 6:30 P.M. Admission is $4; children under 12 are admitted free. Call (717) 928-9259 or (717) 836-5431 for more information.

Frybread

4 cups all-purpose flour	2 cups water
2 tablespoons baking powder	vegetable oil
1 teaspoon salt	

In large bowl, combine flour, baking powder, and salt. Gradually add water until a soft, pliable dough forms. (Dough should not be sticky.) Transfer to lightly floured surface. Knead 5 minutes or until smooth and elastic. Return dough to clean bowl. Cover with damp cloth. Let rise 30 minutes. Shape dough into round balls about the size of eggs. Using floured rolling pin, roll out each ball of dough on lightly floured surface to about ½ inch thickness. (For crisper bread, dough may be rolled slightly thinner.) Pat pieces of dough from hand to hand until each is stretched to a diameter of 8 to 12 inches. Poke a small hole in center of each to allow steam to escape during frying. In large frying pan or saucepan, heat 1½ inches of oil over medium heat until very hot but not smoking. Carefully slip one piece of the dough into the hot oil. Cook until golden brown and puffy. Turn and cook until other side is golden brown. Remove from oil and drain on paper towels. Repeat procedure with remaining dough. Cover with foil and keep warm in low oven until all dough is fried. Serve hot. Makes about 16 frybreads.

Native American Tacos

1½ cups anasazi or other
    small pink or red beans
2 large green bell peppers
6 pieces frybread
olive oil
1½ cups chopped fresh arugula

1 large tomato, sliced
2 ripe avocados, halved
    and sliced
1 red onion, thinly sliced
    and separated into rings

Cover beans with water and soak overnight in refrigerator. Then drain and transfer beans to large saucepan. Cover with fresh water. Bring to boil. Reduce heat and simmer, covered, 2 hours or until very tender. Remove from heat. Drain well and set aside. While beans are cooking, stem, seed, and cut bell peppers in half lengthwise. Place skin side up on rack over broiler pan. Broil a few inches from heat 15 to 20 minutes or until skins blacken all over, watching carefully and turning occasionally while broiling. Transfer to plastic bag and seal tightly. Let stand 15 minutes. Remove from bag. Peel and discard skins. Slice roasted peppers and set aside. Lightly brush frybread with olive oil. Top each piece with ½ cup beans, ¼ cup arugula, tomato and avocado slices, onion rings, and roasted peppers. Serve immediately. Makes 6 servings.

Carlisle, Pennsylvania, maintains a strong Native American legacy as a result of the Indian Industrial School in existence there between 1879 and 1918. More than 10,000 children from hundreds of Indian nations stayed at the school during its operation. There wasn't much Native American cooking going on there, however, since the school's founder, Richard Henry Pratt, believed the children should eat, sleep, and breathe the European-American culture.

Today Carlisle hosts the Jim Thorpe Pow-Wow, named in honor of the great Native American Olympic athlete, who spent part of his childhood at the school. During the last weekend in June, hundreds converge on the Carlisle Fairgrounds to view the customs and crafts of Indian tribes like the Saponi and Tuscarora. In addition to face painting, basketry, pottery, and bow and arrow making, the event offers plenty of Indian food, including frybread tacos and buffalo burgers.

Tickets are $7 per adult, $4 for children and senior citizens. The Jim Thorpe Pow-Wow is relatively new and, as a result, still evolving, so it's best to call (717) 257-5383 for details before venturing to Carlisle.

Near Lake Wallenpaupack in northeastern Pennsylvania, Doris Waller and her family, descendants of the Lenape Indians, host their own Native American Pow-Wow and Western Festival at Mountain Top. Held during the Labor Day weekend, the Mountain Top Pow-Wow has some serious prize money waiting for the best of the fully costumed Native American men, women, and children who participate in various drum and dance competitions. There are also Native American arts and crafts, a teepee raising, western horseback riding, hayrides, and country music.

Native American vendors serve up a host of corn dishes, including chowder, as well as a tasty venison stew, buffalo stew, and buffalo burgers. Frybread is available with the popular taco seasonings, and for a simple dessert or snack, the native bread is sprinkled with cinnamon and sugar.

The Mountain Top Pow-Wow is held on Labor Day weekend from Friday through Monday, from 10 A.M. to 9 P.M. daily. Tickets are $8 per adult, $4 for senior citizens and children under 12. For more information, call the Mountain Top Native American Association at (717) 226-2620.

Watercress Salad

3 tablespoons cider vinegar
1 tablespoon maple syrup
1½ tablespoons safflower oil
salt and coarsely ground
   black pepper, to taste

8 cups washed and
   torn watercress
4 green onions, sliced

In large bowl, whisk together vinegar and maple syrup. Gradually add oil in thin stream, whisking constantly. Salt and pepper to taste. Add watercress and green onions, gently tossing to coat with dressing. Serve immediately. Makes 4 servings.

Al Williams is half Cherokee (and he notes, chuckling, that his "other half" is Swedish). Just after Labor Day, Williams hosts a Native American festival at Wildcat Park, located about an hour east of Erie—one of the most beautiful parks in the nation, according to Williams. Some years ago, the park needed work, so Williams devised the Native American event as a way to raise money to preserve it. His idea worked, and today more than 3,000 people attend the Wildcat Park Native American Festival each year.

Tribes from all parts of the country and the world, including South America, visit Wildcat Park's celebration, but the local Seneca tribe is most involved in the competition dancing and exhibitions intended to educate the public about Native American ways. The Senecas have a reservation not too far from the festival, so if you have time, you can visit them at home, too.

Williams says he's found the country's finest Native American food vendors to host his event. Kathy Mitchell, a Seneca, and Syd Grant, a Cherokee, prepare the Indian cuisine you'll find at Wildcat Park. There's buffalo stew, frybread served with berry jam, and nicely seasoned tacos. Soups, stews, chowders, and succotash made with the "three sisters" are available, too.

The Native American Festival at Wildcat Park is located on Route 6 between Kane and Warren, Pennsylvania. The event runs Friday, Saturday, and Sunday the weekend after Labor Day, from 10 A.M. to 9 P.M. daily. Admission is $5 per adult and $3 per child. Call (814) 362-4068 or 368-9370 for more information.

Wild Rice in Butternut Squash

1 large butternut squash
1 tablespoon corn oil
1½ cups sliced fresh
   shiitake mushrooms
2 cloves garlic, crushed
3 cups cooked wild rice
½ cup chopped, lightly
   toasted walnuts
   (see below)

4 green onions, chopped
2 tablespoons snipped
   fresh parsley
1 tablespoon snipped
   fresh dill
salt and coarsely ground
   black pepper, to taste

Cut squash lengthwise. Scoop out and discard seeds. Place squash, cut side down, in lightly greased 13×9-inch oblong baking dish. Bake at 350 degrees for 1 hour, or until tender. Set aside. Heat oil in large skillet over medium high heat. Add mushrooms and garlic. Sauté 1 to 2 minutes. Stir in cooked wild rice, ⅓ cup of the toasted walnuts, green onions, parsley, and dill. Salt and pepper to taste. Spoon mixture into baked squash halves. Return to baking dish. Sprinkle with remaining toasted walnuts. Cover and bake at 350 degrees for 30 minutes. Remove cover and bake an additional 10 minutes. Serve immediately. Makes 4 servings.

Note: To toast walnuts, arrange in single layer on baking sheet. Bake at 350 degrees for 3 to 5 minutes or just until browned, stirring occasionally. Cool and chop.

Most universities in this country support and promote cultural awareness, and Bloomsburg University is no exception. Although the school does not have an annual Native American celebration, it does hold events on a semiregular basis. I learned about Bloomsburg's Native American Arts and Crafts Show from Al Williams, founder of the Wildcat Park fest. He was on his way to Bloomsburg University to sell his own Indian wares when I interviewed him for this book on an unseasonably warm November day.

Madeline Foshay, part Cherokee and advisor for Bloomsburg University's Native American Cultural Society, explains that the school of

7,000 students has a small but enthusiastic population of Native Americans who belong to the society and put on various events to raise awareness about the Indian's legacy. The Native American Arts and Crafts Show was one of those events, held the year I wrote this book.

The show was held in the university's student union, Kehr Union, just off East Second Street. Along with beautiful and colorful Indian artifacts, leather pieces, and jewelry, there was plenty of food. The vendor was a member of a Canadian tribe called the Micmacs and knew a thing or two about buffalo hot dogs, sausages, and stew. His frybread tacos and succotash (made with the "sister" ingredients) were exceptional.

The Bloomsburg event commanded a modest $2 admission fee for adults, and children under 12 were admitted free. Since Bloomsburg University holds events on a less than yearly basis, it is best to call (717) 389-4574 for a schedule, or write the Native American Cultural Society, Bloomsburg University, Box 124, Kehr Union, 400 E. 2nd St., Bloomsburg, PA 17815.

First Thanksgiving Bean Soup

1 cup dry pinto or anasazi beans
vegetable stock or water
1 medium onion, chopped
1 small red, green, or
   yellow bell pepper, chopped
2 cloves garlic, crushed
½ teaspoon ground cumin
¼ teaspoon ground
   coriander
dash cayenne (red pepper)
salt and coarsely ground
   black pepper, to taste
fresh cilantro leaves

Cover beans with water and soak overnight in refrigerator. Then drain beans, reserving soaking water. Measure soaking water and add enough vegetable broth or additional water to make 6 cups. Transfer to large kettle. Add soaked beans, onion, bell pepper, garlic, cumin, coriander, and cayenne. Bring to boil. Reduce heat and simmer, covered, for 2 hours, or until beans are tender. Salt and pepper to taste. Ladle into soup crocks and garnish with fresh cilantro leaves. Serve immediately. Makes 4 servings.

Succotash

The word succotash comes from the Indian word *misickquatash*, which means corn that has not been crushed or ground. Native Americans taught the colonists to plant corn and beans together as a way to preserve the earth. At harvest time the beans and corn were cooked together, and over generations the recipe was altered and adapted to the varying tastes of the settlers.

¼ cup butter
2 cups fresh or thawed
    frozen corn kernels
2 cups drained canned
    lima beans

½ cup heavy or
    whipping cream
salt and coarsely ground
    black pepper, to taste
snipped fresh flat-leaf
    parsley

In medium saucepan melt butter. Add corn and lima beans. Stir in cream. Bring to a low simmer and cook uncovered, 5 minutes, or just until heated through. Salt and pepper to taste. Garnish with parsley just before serving. Makes 6 servings.

If you would like to learn more about Native American cooking, look for *Spirit of the Harvest: North American Indian Cooking,* by Beverly Cox and Martin Jacobs (Stewart, Tabori, and Chang, 1991). *American Indian Food and Lore,* by Carolyn Niethammer (Collier Books, 1974), gives in-depth explanations of Native American food customs and contains 150 authentic recipes.

Italy

Of Pasta and Pesto

Although Italian immigration to the New World dates back to the voyages of Columbus, the end of the nineteenth century marked the beginning of the most significant movement from Italy to the United States. Seeking political freedom and improved economic status, the first Italian immigrants came from Sicily and southern parts of the country to cities like Philadelphia and Pittsburgh. Some were artists and musicians who eventually moved on, while many others permanently settled their families in the commonwealth.

In the early 1900s, jobs were plentiful in the growing American cities and Italians were able to find work, often holding several jobs at once before settling into permanent careers. In Philadelphia, for example, they worked as barbers, tailors, carpenters, shoemakers, and the like, applying skills they had learned in Italy.

Along with expertise in skilled trades, the Italian immigrants excelled in the kitchen, just as they had in the Old World. Cooks weren't about to sacrifice age-old culinary techniques in order to blend in with the rest of America. Italy's food was her people's heritage.

In Italy, peasants knew plain and simple methods of food preparation. Meals were based on vegetables and grains—peas, beans, corn, tomatoes, onions, and wild herbs. Coarse black bread was a staple. Meat and pasta were often luxuries.

When peasants moved to the United States, they planted small backyard gardens; raised cows, goats, and chickens; and built outdoor brick ovens to simulate Italian cooking methods. As economic conditions improved, pasta, meat, coffee, and sugar became more common, very welcome additions to the dinner table.

The typical Italian-American kitchen houses lots of garlic (aglio), olive oil (olio d'oliva), mushrooms (funghi), nuts (nochi), and ingredients specific to various regions of Italy. Because of the influx of Southern Italian immigrants to the United States, recipes from that region are considered classic Italian cooking. This Neapolitan cuisine, including rich, spicy tomato sauces and pasta, is recognized as the quintessential Italian food. More recently, though, Northern Italian dishes, characterized by rice (risotto), corn (polenta), and buttery bases, have gained popularity and have evolved into modern-day classics like spaghetti, meatballs, and pizza.

"Little Italies" all over the country have provided a safe haven for Italian immigrants, who often faced hostility and prejudice in America.

Within Little Italy, the immigrants established markets, restaurants, and an overall lifestyle that mirrored their culture and provided emotional support.

South Philadelphia has its own version of Little Italy on 9th Street—the Italian Market. Bordered by Christian Street on the north and Federal Street on the south, Philly's Italian Market has evolved from a few Sicilian pushcarts full of wares in the early 1900s to the place to shop and eat in South Philadelphia today.

Many stories surround Little Italy and the Italian Market. Food historians trace the origin of the Philadelphia hoagie to the nonskilled Italian laborers who once worked on Hog Island, just off the coast near South Philadelphia's Market. Italian women would pack lunches—long, crusty loaves of bread filled with salami, provolone cheese, and hot peppers—for their husbands who worked on Hog Island. These men were nicknamed "Hoggies," and as a result, their hearty lunchtime sandwich became known as the hoagie.

Shopping South Philadelphia's Italian Market can be quite informative. Take Anastasi Seafood, for example. Co-owner Janet Stechman knows fresh fish and wants to educate her customers about it, too. Stechman answers any question, offering tips on selecting, storing, and cooking fresh seafood. At Anastasi's, you can choose from farm-raised rainbow trout, salmon, clams, mussels, and catfish, as well as prepared items like ready-to-cook stuffed seafood and crab cakes. Every item is fresh, fresh, fresh. Anastasi Seafood, located at 905 and 1035 S. 9th St., is open every day except Monday. Call (215) 922-4828 for more information.

Claudio Auriemma, known as the "king of cheese," opened Claudio's in the Italian Market during the early 1960s, and today his sons still pack and sell the best imported cheeses, olive oils, and pasta under the Claudio name. This is the place to shop for all kinds of authentic Italian groceries. Claudio's is located at 924–26 S. 9th St. and is open seven days a week. Call (215) 627-1873 for information.

Cousins Emilio and William Mignucci operate the Di Bruno Brothers Delicatessen just up the street from Claudio's. "Foodies" claim that this place offers the widest variety of Italian foods and ingredients in the Delaware Valley. You'll find fresh mozzarella (called scamorza in the old days) and roasted peppers made daily, homemade soppressetta (cured and dry-aged sausage), and an exceptional imported pasta called CaraNora. Di Bruno's has an unusual assortment of gourmet items, including roasted artichokes with sun-dried tomatoes, stuffed cherry peppers with olives and anchovies, and eleven homemade cheese spreads made by "Uncle Danny." Di Bruno Brothers is located at 930 S. 9th St. and is open seven days a week. Call (215) 922-2876 for information.

The best chefs in Philadelphia go to Michael Anastasio Produce for fruits and vegetables, because Michael has the freshest and the best variety. You'll find an impressive selection of hard-to-find items, like Italian blood oranges, miniature vegetables, and truffles. You don't have to be a chef to go there, however. Retail customers are welcome but should try to shop on Saturdays or weekday afternoons to avoid the wholesale rush. Michael's is closed Sunday. If your shopping list is long, you can drop it off or call ahead and let Michael's crew bag the items for you. Michael Anastasio Produce is located at 911 Christian St., telephone (215) 627-2807.

Around the corner on Christian Street, you'll find Litto's Bakery & Cafe, well worth a morning walk if you're in the mood for really good, homemade Italian pastry. The bakery was opened in 1932, with Grandfather Orazio waiting on customers while his son, Joe Litto, Sr., baked his popular wedding cakes and cannoli. Grandmother Josephine was the bakery's very successful marketer, selling items up and down Germantown Avenue via the trolley. Nowadays, Joe Litto, Jr., continues the tradition, making ricotta pie, canaille with three fillings, and items like polenta, porridge, and fritatta for the on-premises café. Litto's is at 910 Christian St. and is open every day except Monday. Call (215) 627-7037 for more information.

South Philly's merchants sponsor the Italian Market Festival on the third Sunday in May every year. The event opens with a procession given by St. Paul's Catholic Church and continues throughout the day with games, contests, music, and of course, lots of Italian food. There's also a relatively new festival held in the fall with a canaille-eating competition, a pasta sauce recipe contest, and plenty of Italian food samples. A monthly special-interest newspaper called *Phillyfeast* lists South Philadelphia's food events and is available throughout the city and surrounding area.

Louise Cianfero Simpson started toddling to Philadelphia's Italian Market when she was 5 and has been going there ever since. If you don't know much about the Market but would like to learn, call on Louise. She started guided tours of the Italian Market in 1991 with the help of her sister, and they named the business Sorelle Cianfero, meaning "the Cianfero sisters."

Simpson's Italian Market tours are educational. Want to find an exotic ingredient for that new Italian recipe? Ask Louise. She can also tell you how to select the right olive oil and why good balsamic vine-gar costs more than a bottle of vintage wine. To find out more about the tours offered by Sorelle Cianfero, call (215) 772-0739.

Zucchini con Pomodori
(Zucchini with Sun-Dried Tomatoes)

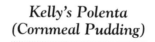

10 sun-dried tomatoes (not packed in oil), chopped	2 cloves garlic, minced
	2 pounds fresh zucchini, thinly sliced (do not peel)
¼ cup hot water	
¼ cup olive oil	salt and coarsely ground
1 medium onion, chopped	black pepper, to taste

Soak tomatoes in hot water for 20 minutes (do not drain). Meanwhile, in large skillet, heat olive oil over medium heat. Add onion and garlic. Sauté 3 minutes or until onion is soft. Add zucchini. Sauté 5 minutes more. Stir in tomatoes and soaking liquid. Salt and pepper to taste. Heat through. Serve immediately. Makes 6 servings.

Kelly's Polenta
(Cornmeal Pudding)

4 cups water	1 teaspoon salt
1 cup yellow cornmeal	

In large saucepan, bring water to boil. Gradually add cornmeal, stirring constantly with wire whisk. Stir in salt. Reduce heat to medium. Cook 45 minutes or until thick and softened, stirring frequently. Serve hot as a side dish. Makes 4 to 6 servings.

Thicker Variation: Bring 4 cups water and 2 teaspoons salt to full boil in large, heavy skillet. Gradually add 2 cups yellow cornmeal with wire whisk, stirring until moistened. Reduce heat to lowest temperature and smooth top to make even. Cook, uncovered, 20 minutes or until edge begins to form crust and center is firm. (Do not stir while cooking.) Serve hot from pan or invert onto serving plate and slice. Makes 6 to 8 servings.

Italian immigrants weren't drawn just to Pennsylvania's cities; many started businesses near the coal regions and rail systems around Scranton, Wilkes-Barre, Hazleton, and Altoona. There were silk makers, stone masons, tinsmiths, and marble cutters. Others sold produce, ran hotels, and started restaurants. Those without marketable skills worked in the mines and railroads. While these industries thrived, so did the Italian immigrants who lived nearby.

It's probably not too surprising to find one of Pennsylvania's largest Italian food events about 10 miles north of Altoona on Route 220. That's where you'll find a quaint little town called Tipton, home of the Blands Park Italian Food Festival.

On a Sunday in September, Blands Amusement Park invites several area food vendors to cook up their best Italian dishes and serve them to the hungry masses . . . and I do mean masses—the festival draws thousands of people eager to sample classic Italian fare prepared by clubs, churches, restaurants, and Blands's own food service department.

Blands's food service director, John McCrackin, takes care of the festival details with lots of support from his quality-conscious staff. "Everything is made from scratch here," says John. "We're very particular and use our own recipes for ingredients like the meatballs and sausage." However, Chef John also explains that Del Grosso Foods, a big-name pasta sauce company, is nearby and he'd better use its sauce or he's in trouble. Del Grosso helps sponsor the Blands Park event.

Although the festival menu varies somewhat from year to year, John and his crew make strictly Italian fare like lasagna, gnocchi (potato dumplings), chicken and eggplant Parmesan, and a tasty wedding soup. You can get crusty bread and a green salad to go with your entree and probably won't pay more than $6 for an entire meal. Other vendors round out the Blands Park festival menu with their own Italian creations— chicken cacciatore, pasta e fagioli, sweet baked treats like rum cake and cannoli, and just about any other Italian dish you've ever dreamed of eating.

Blands Park holds its festival the third Sunday in September and charges no admission. For more information, call (814) 684-3538.

Italian Wedding Soup

4 quarts cold water
4-pound stewing chicken
4 stalks celery with tops, chopped
1 medium onion, chopped
¼ cup snipped fresh parsley
½ pound ground beef
1 teaspoon fine, dry Italian-
  seasoned bread crumbs
half of 10-ounce package
  frozen spinach, thawed
  and drained

½ cup ancini de pepe
  (small noodles),
  uncooked
4 eggs
¼ cup all-purpose flour
¼ cup freshly grated
  Parmesan cheese
3 chicken bouillon cubes
salt and coarsely ground
  black pepper, to taste
vegetable oil cooking spray

In large kettle or Dutch oven, combine cold water, chicken, celery, onion, and parsley. Cover and bring to boil over medium high heat. Reduce heat to medium low and simmer 1 hour, covered, stirring occasionally. Meanwhile, combine ground beef and bread crumbs. Add just enough of the cooking broth from the chicken to moisten the meat mixture. Roll into tiny meatballs, not more than ½ inch wide. Lightly brown in large skillet that has been coated with cooking spray. Set aside. Remove cooked chicken from broth, reserving broth for soup. Remove and discard chicken skin and bones. Cut meat into small pieces. Increase heat under broth to medium high. Add chicken, spinach, uncooked ancini de pepe, and browned meatballs. Bring to boil. Boil and stir 2 minutes. In small bowl, beat eggs slightly. Whisk in flour and Parmesan cheese. Gradually add to boiling soup, whisking constantly. Boil and whisk 2 minutes. Stir in bouillon cubes, stirring until dissolved. Salt and pepper to taste. Serve hot. Makes 6 to 8 servings.

Parmigiana di Melanzane
(Eggplant Parmesan)

2 pounds eggplant, peeled and
   sliced ½ inch thick
salt
tomato sauce (below)
all-purpose flour
olive oil
2 cups shredded mozzarella cheese

⅓ cup freshly grated
   Parmesan cheese
coarsely ground black
   pepper, to taste
fresh basil leaves

Sprinkle eggplant with salt. Set aside 1 hour to drain. Meanwhile, prepare tomato sauce and set aside. Pat dry eggplant slices with clean paper towels. Dredge through flour until lightly coated. In large skillet, heat just enough olive oil to coat bottom of pan over medium heat. Arrange eggplant in single layer in skillet. Cover and cook until bottoms are very lightly browned. Turn and continue cooking until other side is lightly browned. Transfer to paper-towel-lined plate and repeat cooking procedure with remaining eggplant. Spread small amount of tomato sauce in bottom of lightly greased 13×9-inch pan. Arrange layer of eggplant over top. Sprinkle with some of the mozzarella and Parmesan cheeses. Salt and pepper to taste. Spoon on another layer of tomato sauce. Repeat layers, ending with sauce and a sprinkling of Parmesan cheese. Bake at 350 degrees for 45 minutes. Garnish with fresh basil and serve hot. Makes 4 to 6 servings.

   Tomato Sauce: In medium saucepan, heat ¼ cup olive oil over medium heat. Add 1 finely chopped onion. Sauté 6 minutes or until translucent. Add 1 can whole tomatoes (16-ounce size) with liquid, 1 clove minced garlic, 1 tablespoon snipped fresh basil, and 1 teaspoon snipped fresh oregano. Salt and pepper to taste. If desired, add a dash of cayenne (ground red pepper). Cover and simmer 30 minutes, stirring occasionally. Puree in food processor.

Scranton hosts its own Italian festival, La Festa Italiana, on the court-house square every Labor Day weekend. Framed by Spruce and Linden Streets and Adams and Washington Avenues, the Lackawanna County

Courthouse looks like the center of an Italian market. Oh, there are some nonfood attractions, like pony rides, kids' games, and handicrafts, but the singing, dancing, and eats are sheer Italian.

Based on the number of vendors I saw peddling America's favorite Italian pie, Scranton should be the pizza capital of the world. Although unsubstantiated, I think it's fair to say there are more slices of pizza per capita in that town than there are trains—and there are a lot of trains in Scranton. There was also stromboli, which is really pizza with Italian meat and cheese rolled up and baked. The calzone was similar to stromboli, but folded to create a half circle. Calzone is a specialty of Naples, and the word literally means "trouser leg," since the shape resembles the baggy pants worn by Neapolitan men more than a century ago. The pizza I tasted in Scranton—in any shape or form—was delicious.

There were various forms of classic pasta with herbed tomato sauces and Italian cheeses—spaghetti, lasagna, stuffed shells, and ziti, to name some. If it hadn't been so hot, I would have tried the pasta e fagioli, that hearty pasta and bean soup in tomato broth. Several vendors sold something called porketta, which was simply pork cooked in a seasoned broth, sliced, and served on a hard roll, similar to a Philadelphia cheesesteak sandwich. I asked one of the vendors about the specific seasoning blend he used for porketta. He wouldn't reveal his recipe, telling me it was a secret.

Polenta is a popular item at Scranton's La Festa Italiana and a common dish in Northern Italy. It usually replaces bread, potatoes, or other starchy dishes. Polenta is made with yellow cornmeal (white is virtually unknown in Italy) and is served a number of ways—sliced, baked, or fried like mush.

With a passion for excellent pastry, I was drawn to the tent that shaded cannoli from the hot sun. Cannoli is a ricotta-cream-filled pastry that only Italians really know how to make well. There were dozens of other Italian pastries to pick from, including biscotti, those crisp but not-too-sweet crescents so popular with espresso.

La Festa Italiana runs from noon till about 9 P.M., Saturday, Sunday, and Monday over the Labor Day weekend. Food prices are very reasonable, and so is the parking. The Steamtown Mall and train museum are also within walking distance of the festival. For more information, call (717) 344-7411 or (717) 346-6384.

Michael's Pasta e Fagioli
(Pasta and Bean Soup)

2 cups dry kidney beans
cold water
3 tablespoons olive oil
2 slices uncooked bacon,
   cut into thin strips
1 small onion, minced
1 stalk celery, minced
1 clove garlic, crushed
4 plum tomatoes, chopped

2 quarts hot water
2 teaspoons salt
dash coarsely ground
   black pepper
2 cups macaroni or other
   small pasta, uncooked
¼ cup freshly grated
   Romano cheese
fresh basil leaves

Cover beans with cold water. Bring to boil. Cook 2 minutes. Turn off heat and let stand 1 hour. Return to boil. Reduce heat and simmer 1½ hours or until tender. Drain and set aside. In kettle or Dutch oven, heat olive oil over medium heat. Add bacon, onion, celery, and garlic. Sauté 5 minutes or until lightly browned. Add tomatoes and continue cooking 3 minutes or until softened, stirring constantly. Stir in hot water, cooked and drained beans, salt, and pepper. Bring to boil. Add pasta. Cook 8 to 10 minutes or until pasta is al dente, stirring frequently. (Add small amount of additional water, as needed, for desired consistency.) Ladle into serving bowls. Sprinkle with Romano cheese and garnish with fresh basil. Serve immediately. Makes 6 to 8 servings.

Focaccia

1 package active dry yeast
1 cup warm (not hot) water
⅛ teaspoon sugar
3 to 3½ cups unbleached
   all-purpose flour

1 teaspoon salt
3 tablespoons olive
   oil, divided
coarse salt

In large, warm bowl, sprinkle yeast over warm water. Stir in sugar. Let stand 5 to 10 minutes or until sugar dissolves and mixture foams. Stir in 1 cup of the flour and 1 teaspoon salt. Add another cup flour, mixing with wooden spoon until dough begins to pull away from side of bowl. Turn out onto lightly floured surface. Gradually knead in additional flour as needed to form moist (not too sticky) dough. Knead 8 to 10 minutes, or until dough is smooth and elastic. Shape into smooth ball. Place in lightly oiled bowl, turning to lightly coat dough with oil. Cover with clean, damp cloth. Let rise in warm place at least 45 minutes or until doubled in volume. Punch down dough with fist. Knead 3 to 4 minutes. Brush large baking sheet with 1 tablespoon of the olive oil. Using lightly oiled fingers, press dough out to about 1 inch thickness in prepared pan. Cover loosely with damp cloth. Let rise in warm place 30 minutes. Using fingertips, gently press indentations in rows at about 2½-inch intervals into surface of dough. Brush with remaining 2 tablespoons olive oil. Sprinkle with coarse salt, to taste. Bake at 400 degrees for 25 minutes or until lightly browned. Cut into squares and serve warm or at room temperature. Makes 6 to 8 servings.

Note: Focaccia also makes an excellent pizza crust. Just add tomato sauce and toppings before baking.

Since 1976, the Italian Heritage Council of Berks County has hosted one of Pennsylvania's most popular festivals, called the Italian Heritage Festival. Close to 4,000 people are drawn to the Reading Memorial Stadium on a September weekend to experience extraordinary Italian cuisine and culture. This is a family-oriented event that includes a "Little Miss Italy" contest, fabulous display of Italian cars, soccer matches, and bocce tournaments, as well as high-energy folkdancing and music.

The fall weather is usually perfect for a stroll from booth to booth to enjoy Italian classics like manicotti, baked ziti, and lots of variations on pizza. There's abundant homemade pastry, too, made with rich and creamy fillings and flaky crusts worthy of taking home. The food is inexpensive and most is made from scratch by area vendors.

The Italian Heritage Festival is held on one Sunday in mid-September. There is no admission or fee for parking. For more information, call (610) 929-2977.

Daddy's Calzone

focaccia dough
(see preceding recipe)
1½ cups ricotta cheese
1 cup shredded mozzarella
cheese
¾ cup finely diced cooked
Italian ham
¼ cup freshly grated
Parmesan cheese

8 plum tomatoes, peeled
and diced
2 tablespoons snipped
fresh basil
salt and coarsely ground
black pepper, to taste
olive oil

Allow focaccia dough to rise first time according to directions. Punch down and knead lightly on floured surface. Divide into 4 equal portions. Shape each into smooth ball. Using floured rolling pin, roll out each ball of dough ¼ inch thick on lightly floured surface. Set aside. In large bowl, combine ricotta cheese, mozzarella cheese, ham, Parmesan cheese, tomatoes, basil, salt, and pepper. Divide evenly among the 4 circles of dough, spooning mixture on half of each circle and leaving a 1-inch border. Fold unfilled half of each circle up and over filling, bringing edges of dough together. Crimp edges with back of fork to seal shut. Arrange on lightly oiled baking sheet. Brush tops with olive oil. Bake at 475 degrees for 15 to 20 minutes or until puffy and golden brown. Makes 4 servings.

Cannoli (Cream-Filled Pastry)

3 cups sifted all-purpose flour
3 tablespoons melted butter
1 tablespoon sugar
⅛ teaspoon salt
⅔ to ¾ cup red wine

1 egg yolk, slightly beaten
vegetable oil
ricotta filling (below)
finely chopped
    pistachio nuts

In large bowl, combine flour, melted butter, sugar, and salt. Gradually add enough of the wine to make stiff dough. Knead on lightly floured surface 15 minutes, or until smooth and soft, adding small amount of additional flour as needed to prevent sticking. Shape into ball. Wrap in plastic wrap or waxed paper. Refrigerate 1 hour. Then divide into 2 equal portions and shape into balls. Using floured rolling pin, roll each ball paper-thin on lightly floured surface. Cut into 4-inch squares. Place cannoli tube diagonally from corner to opposite corner across each square. Overlap opposite corners of dough, wrapping around tube. Brush corners with beaten egg yolk. Gently press together to seal. In large saucepan, heat about 3 inches vegetable oil to 390 degrees. Fry 2 to 3 cannoli at a time until golden brown, turning occasionally. Using tongs, remove to paper-towel-lined tray to drain. Repeat frying procedure with remaining dough. Cool completely and carefully remove tubes. Just before serving, stuff ricotta filling into cooled tubes using small spoon. Dip ends into chopped pistachio nuts. Serve immediately. Makes about 2 dozen.

Note: Pastry will get soggy if filled in advance. Unfilled cannoli may be prepared several weeks in advance of filling. Store in cool, dry place.

Ricotta Filling: In large bowl, beat 3 pounds ricotta cheese for 2 minutes. Blend in ¼ cup confectioner's sugar and ¼ cup any flavor sweet liqueur. Stir in 3 tablespoons grated bittersweet chocolate and 1 tablespoon minced candied orange peel. Cover and refrigerate until ready to use. Filling may be made up to 3 days in advance.

I love a bargain and was excited to find a wonderful Italian cookbook with full-color pages and easy-to-follow recipes for just $10 at my neighborhood discount store. The cookbook, called *The Best of Italian Regional Cooking* (Anness Publishing Limited, 1995), is by Carla Capalbo and usually retails for $35. I also like a no-frills book called *The Little Italian Cookbook*, by Christiana Lindsay and Alfred Lepore (Walker and Company, 1968). It's the first Italian cookbook I ever bought and cost just $4 in the early seventies.

Linguine con Pesto
(Linguine with Pesto Sauce)

¾ cup snipped fresh basil leaves
¼ cup olive oil
4 cloves garlic
3 tablespoons pine nuts
1 tablespoon melted butter
½ teaspoon salt
½ cup freshly grated
   Parmesan cheese

¼ cup freshly grated
   Pecorino cheese
coarsely ground black
   pepper, to taste
1¼ pounds linguine,
   uncooked

In food processor, place basil, olive oil, garlic, pine nuts, butter, and salt. Process until smooth. Stir in cheeses. Add pepper to taste. Set aside. Cook linguine according to package directions. Drain, adding ¼ cup of the cooking water to the sauce. Toss drained pasta with sauce. Serve immediately. Makes 6 servings.

Penne con Tonno e Mozzarella
(Penne with Tuna and Mozzarella)

1 pound penne, uncooked
1 can (6 ounces) tuna packed in spring water, drained
3 tablespoons snipped fresh flat-leaf Italian parsley
1 tablespoon drained and rinsed capers, minced

2 cloves garlic, minced
⅓ cup olive oil
salt and coarsely ground black pepper, to taste
⅔ cup shredded mozzarella cheese

Cook penne according to package directions. Drain and keep warm. In medium bowl, combine tuna, parsley, capers, and garlic. Toss with olive oil. Add salt and pepper to taste. Add to warm pasta, gently tossing. Sprinkle with mozzarella cheese. Serve immediately. Makes 4 servings.

Mushroom Bruschetta

1 medium loaf Italian bread, halved crosswise
½ cup olive oil, divided
1½ pounds fresh mushrooms such as shiitake, chanterelle, or oyster, sliced

12 cloves garlic, thinly sliced
1½ cups dry white wine
salt and coarsely ground black pepper, to taste
½ cup snipped fresh marjoram

Cut bread into ½-inch-thick slices. Arrange on large baking sheet. Brush with 3 tablespoons of the olive oil. Bake at 375 degrees for 8 to 10 minutes, or until lightly toasted. Set aside. In large skillet, heat remaining 5 tablespoons olive oil over medium low heat. Add mushrooms and garlic and sauté 5 minutes. Increase heat to medium high. Add wine and bring to boil. Reduce heat and simmer 15 to 20 minutes, or until liquid is evaporated, stirring occasionally. Salt and pepper to taste. Add marjoram. Spoon mixture over toast. Serve immediately or at room temperature. Makes about 2 dozen.

Tiramisu ("Pick Me Up" Coffee Dessert)

about 24 sponge-cake
   ladyfingers, split
about ⅓ cup coffee-flavored
   liqueur or espresso coffee
6 fresh egg yolks
1¼ cups sugar

1¼ cups mascarpone
   cheese (see note)
1¾ cups heavy or
   whipping cream
grated bittersweet chocolate
sweetened whipped cream
   (below)

Arrange ladyfinger halves, split sides up, on bottom and around side of 3-quart soufflé dish. Generously brush with liqueur or espresso. Set aside. In top of double boiler or heatproof bowl, beat egg yolks and sugar 1 to 2 minutes or until thickened and light in color. Place over hot (not boiling) water. Cook 10 minutes, stirring or whisking constantly. Remove from heat. Beat in mascarpone cheese. In small bowl, beat cream until soft peaks form. Fold into egg yolk mixture. Spoon half of mixture into ladyfinger-lined dish. Arrange single layer of ladyfinger halves over top. Brush with liqueur or espresso. Top with remaining egg yolk mixture. Sprinkle with grated chocolate. Garnish with sweetened whipped cream. Cover and refrigerate several hours or overnight. Makes 10 to 12 servings.

Sweetened Whipped Cream: In small mixer bowl, beat ¾ cup heavy or whipping cream, 1 tablespoon confectioner's sugar, and ¼ teaspoon vanilla extract until soft peaks form. Cover and refrigerate until ready to use.

Note: Mascarpone cheese is a soft cheese similar to cream cheese. It is available in most grocery stores and specialty food shops.

France

Can They Cook!

When Thomas Jefferson returned to Philadelphia in 1789 after four years in France, he brought home cherished recipes for French dishes and an impressive stock of wines. Jefferson entertained often, and inspired by his love of the French lifestyle, managed to work at least some French influence into his dinner parties.

Rich French sauces and desserts were common fare in the Jefferson home. Guests were treated to piquante, Robert, tournée, and hachée sauces and, for dessert, scoops of ice cream in warm pastry shells—probably a forerunner to baked Alaska. Jefferson served his own home-grown vegetables and fruits, French-style, and was likely to end a banquet with floating island, meringues, macaroons, or blanc mange. Jefferson was the first to admit that such meals were quite pretentious and described them as "sinful feasts."

In spite of his love of rich food, Jefferson also learned healthful eating habits from the French, who believed, as nutritionists do today, that Americans ate too much meat and not enough vegetables. Clearly the French, as well as Jefferson, were ahead of their time.

When the French first migrated to the New World, the wilderness lifestyle forced them to simplify their customary food preparation. One-kettle meals of hash, stew, or soup and bread were the usual fare for the voyageurs, who were probably grateful for food in any form. With time and the taming of the wilderness, more complex French cooking techniques reemerged—the preparation of rich sauces and pastries, liberal use of herbs and wine, and artful table presentations.

As the French settled down and began to make themselves at home in the colonies, breadmaking became an integral part of routine kitchen chores. Large, round loaves called miches, or "common bread," were served at every meal. Leftover bread was "recycled" into French toast—stale bread slices were dipped in a mixture of egg and milk, then fried in butter. (This recipe hasn't changed much over the years and still tastes best made with thick slices of French bread.)

French food became popular among other ethnic groups. The English and Germans enjoyed omelets, French dressing, onion soup, French fries, and éclairs and blended these recipes with their own to create one-of-a-kind dishes that varied from one family to the next. There were, however, skeptics who viewed French cooking as much too rich and stayed with their simpler colonial eating habits.

Jefferson Hollandaise Sauce

¼ cup unsalted (sweet) butter   ½ teaspoon salt
3 egg yolks   dash coarsely ground
1 tablespoon cold water   black pepper
1 tablespoon fresh lemon juice   dash cayenne (red pepper)

In small saucepan, melt butter over low heat. (Do not boil.) Skim off and discard any foam. Set aside. In top of double boiler, whisk together egg yolks, water, lemon juice, salt, black pepper, and cayenne. Place over simmering water. Whisk constantly until mixture thickens. Remove from heat. Gradually add melted butter, a few drops at a time at first, whisking constantly. Continue adding butter in a thin stream, whisking constantly. Stop adding butter when milky solids are visible in bottom of butter pan. Serve immediately over steamed vegetables, roasted meat, or omelets. Makes 6 servings.

The French Azilum in Towanda probably best represents the efforts of the French to settle in Pennsylvania. The French settled at the azilum, or refuge, in the fall of 1793 to escape death or, at the very least, imprisonment at the hands of the Revolutionists back in their homeland. Some even believed that Marie Antoinette, the queen of France, and her two children would escape to the Pennsylvania-based azilum for protection, if necessary.

Earlier, rich and influential Philadelphians had seen the plight of the French refugees as an opportunity to profit and sold the French 600 acres of northern Pennsylvania wilderness, which became the azilum. Within that desolate area, the immigrants built a 300-acre town with a large market square, several shops, a school, a church, and a theater. Houses sprang up, gardens were planted, and dairy farming prospered. The French became entrepreneurs, building a blacksmith shop, gristmill, distillery, and potash factory.

Although the houses of the azilum were primitive, they did include small comforts such as shuttered windows, chimneys, porches, and wallpaper. The occupants made every effort to perpetuate their love of good food in their crude but functional kitchens.

Pat Zalinski, site manager at the French Azilum, says that the French brought dandelions, sorrel, and other herbs with them. They fished for shad in the river and salted the fillets to preserve them. They also raised sheep and brought cattle from France to breed here for milk and cheese.

During the late 1790s, many of the azilum émigrés headed south to warmer climates. With Napoleon's blessing, others returned home. A few families, including the D'Autremonts, LaPortes, Homets, LeFevres, and Brevosts, stayed in Pennsylvania, but the overall result was the disappearance of the azilum altogether by 1803.

Today, not one of the original azilum structures remains. However, French Azilum, Inc., offers tours of the grounds and the second-generation LaPorte House, built in 1836 and owned by the son of an original azilum resident. Unlike the modest cooking areas of the original cabins, the LaPorte House kitchen includes a brick bake oven and a second, portable stove that was carried to picnics and town gatherings. A cast-iron waffle iron engraved with a fleur de lis, a symbol of nobility among the French upper class of the time, is displayed along with demitasse cups and spouted cups for drinking in bed. A butler's fallfront, an elaborate serving cart, stands in the dining room.

A stone-walled wine and root cellar survived the original French village. Excavation in the mid-1950s revealed wine bottles, glass, and ironware. Apparently, the area served as a wine cellar for one of fifty houses in the area and helped confirm the image of the French as wine connoisseurs. Artifacts from the cellar were moved to the museum for display.

Regional Native Americans taught the French settlers how to plant corn and potatoes and to draw maple syrup from nearby trees. In addition to creating lucrative businesses for the site, this produce inspired ideas for bread, main dishes, and desserts prepared with a classic French influence.

The following contemporary French potato side dish could easily have been prepared at French Azilum during the late part of the eighteenth century.

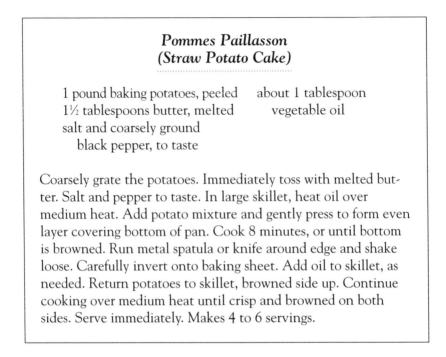

Pommes Paillasson
(Straw Potato Cake)

1 pound baking potatoes, peeled   about 1 tablespoon
1½ tablespoons butter, melted   vegetable oil
salt and coarsely ground
   black pepper, to taste

Coarsely grate the potatoes. Immediately toss with melted butter. Salt and pepper to taste. In large skillet, heat oil over medium heat. Add potato mixture and gently press to form even layer covering bottom of pan. Cook 8 minutes, or until bottom is browned. Run metal spatula or knife around edge and shake loose. Carefully invert onto baking sheet. Add oil to skillet, as needed. Return potatoes to skillet, browned side up. Continue cooking over medium heat until crisp and browned on both sides. Serve immediately. Makes 4 to 6 servings.

The French Azilum is open from June 1 to August 31 but is closed on Mondays and Tuesdays. It is also open weekends during May, September, and October. Admission is $3.50 for adults, $3 for senior citizens, and $2 for students. Preschoolers and members are admitted free. For more information, call (717) 265-3376 or write R.D. 2, Box 266, Towanda, PA 18848.

A FRENCH COOKING GLOSSARY

bain-marie: baking pan or dish set in a larger pan of water; allows food to cook without damage from direct heat

beurre manié: thickener made from equal parts flour and water whisked into cooking liquid

bouquet garni: tied bundle of herbs added to cooking liquid for flavor, then removed before serving

coulis: a fruit or vegetable puree used as a sauce

gratiné: to impart a crisp, browned surface to a baked dish

herbes de Provence: blend of dried herbs that grow wild; usually consists of thyme, marjoram, summer savory, and oregano

julienne: to cut thin, matchstick-shaped pieces of meat or vegetables

papillate: a parchment paper enclosure for cooking food

roux: cooked mixture of flour and fat used to thicken sauces and soups

sauté: to fry quickly over high heat in small amount of fat such as butter

Philadelphia's French School and Cultural Center (Alliance Française de Philadelphia) offers more than a little bit of France without the inconvenience of jet lag. Students at the center learn the language and culture of one of the world's most romantic countries from an impressive faculty striving to "foster a positive relationship between French and American peoples."

Philadelphia's French Alliance, along with people in other parts of the state, country, and France, celebrate Bastille Day on July 14. Bastille Day commemorates the uprising that destroyed a major symbol of oppression in Paris, which led to the formation of the First Republic in France in 1789.

"La Fête de la Bastille" at the Alliance Center in Philadelphia is no ordinary party. The beautifully renovated Bourse Building (between Market and Chestnut Streets) provides a romantic setting for the Bastille Day event. It's a dressy affair with music, dancing, and an expansive French buffet provided by Renaissance Catering, Inc., in Chester Springs.

Patrick Boudou, the young classic French chef who owns and operates Renaissance Catering, has worked at his craft for ten years now in some very romantic parts of the world, including France, Germany, Spain, and the Caribbean. For the last few years, he's proudly claimed Philadelphia's French Alliance as a client.

A FRENCH ALLIANCE BASTILLE DAY MENU

Pain Surprise aux Trois Mousses (Miniature Sandwiches of Shrimp, Tuna, and Salmon Mousse served in Fresh Country French Bread Loaf)

Pain Surprise à la Campagnarde (Miniature Sandwiches of Black Forest Ham, Prosciutto, Pâté, and Saucisson served in Country French Herb Bread Loaf)

Assortiement de Terrines et Condiements (Assorted Pâtés and Condiments)

Saumon Poché Froid en Bellevue, Sauce a l'Aneth Citronnée (Whole Poached Salmon, served chilled in a Citrus-Dill Sauce)

Taboulé Provencale à la Menthe Fraîche servis dañs son Panier (Tabouleh with Fresh Mint served in Individual Tomato Baskets)

Salade "Justine" au Salpicon de Poulet (Breast of Chicken Salad with Red Bliss Potatoes, Shallots, Walnuts, Red and Green Grapes)

Salade Verte composée, Vinaigrette au Balsamic et Basilic Frais (Mesclun Greens in a Balsamic and Fresh Basil Vinaigrette)

Plâteau de Fromages Variés (Assortment of Fine French Cheeses)

Entremet à la Mousseline de Vanille et Fraises Fraiches (Fresh Strawberries and Vanilla Mousse between Layers of Genoise)

Café et Assortiement de Biscuits Sucrés (Coffee and Cookies)

Philadelphia's French Alliance also hosts a masked ball on Mardi Gras ("Fat Tuesday"), the "last fling" in February that precedes the religious observance of Lent. According to tradition, Mardi Gras is the time to don a flashy outfit and mask, act crazy, and pig out. Mardi Gras is a wonderful celebration, and if you can't make the one in New Orleans, the French Alliance in Philadelphia offers an excellent alternative.

The Alliance Française hosts the Bastille Day celebration each year in mid-July and the Mardi Gras Ball each February. For more information, call the Alliance Française at (215) 735-5283. For information on Renaissance Catering, call (610) 933-7107.

Fricassée de Lapin au Thym
(Rabbit-Thyme Casserole)

¼ cup all-purpose flour
salt and coarsely ground
   black pepper, to taste
2½ pounds rabbit, cut up
1 tablespoon butter
1 tablespoon olive oil
1 cup dry red wine

1¼ cups chicken broth
1 tablespoon snipped fresh
   thyme or 1 teaspoon
   dried thyme
1 bay leaf
2 cloves garlic, minced
1 tablespoon Dijon mustard

In shallow bowl, combine flour, salt, and pepper. Dredge rabbit
pieces through flour mixture, coating well. In large, heatproof
casserole dish, melt butter with olive oil over medium high heat.
Add rabbit. Cook until golden brown all over, turning often.
Add wine. Boil 1 minute. Reduce heat. Add chicken broth,
thyme, bay leaf, and garlic. Cover and simmer 1 hour, or until
rabbit is very tender and juices run clear. Stir in mustard.
Arrange rabbit on serving platter. Remove and discard bay leaf
from sauce. Spoon some of sauce over rabbit. Serve remainder
on side. Makes 4 servings.

Salade de Mesclun
(Mixed Green Salad)

1 clove garlic
2 tablespoons red wine vinegar
1 teaspoon Dijon mustard
¼ teaspoon salt
⅛ teaspoon coarsely ground
   black pepper
½ cup extra-virgin olive oil

about 8 ounces cleaned
   and torn mixed salad
   greens, such as curly
   endive, arugula, and
   romaine, and herbs such
   as basil, parsley, and
   tarragon
croutons

Rub large salad bowl with garlic, and leave in bowl. Add vinegar, mustard, salt, and pepper, whisking well. Gradually add
olive oil, whisking constantly. Remove and discard garlic clove.
Add greens and herbs. Toss well. Serve immediately, topped
with croutons. Makes 4 to 6 servings.

Coq au Vin
(Chicken in Red Wine)

1 chicken (about 4 pounds),
   cut into pieces
salt and coarsely ground black
   pepper, to taste
1 tablespoon butter
2 cups mushrooms, quartered
2 tablespoons olive oil

½ pound fresh pearl onions
2 tablespoons
   all-purpose flour
3 cups dry red wine
1 cup chicken broth
bouquet garni (below)
vegetable oil cooking spray

Pat chicken dry with clean paper towels and sprinkle with salt and pepper. Arrange skin side down in large skillet that has been lightly coated with cooking spray. Cook over medium heat 10 to 12 minutes, or until lightly browned, turning at least once. Remove from skillet and set aside. In same skillet, melt butter over medium heat. Add mushrooms and sauté just until golden brown. Set aside. In large, heatproof casserole dish, heat olive oil over medium heat. Add onions. Cover and cook just until browned, stirring frequently. Sprinkle with flour. Cook and stir 2 minutes. Stir in wine. Boil and stir 1 minute. Add chicken, mushrooms, chicken broth, and bouquet garni and bring to boil. Reduce heat to very low. Cover and bake at 325 degrees for 45 minutes, or until chicken is tender and juices run clear. Remove bouquet garni. Transfer chicken and vegetables to plate. Strain cooking liquid, skim fat, and return to dish. Boil cooking liquid until reduced by a third. Return chicken and vegetables to cooking liquid. Heat through. Serve immediately. Makes 4 servings.

   Bouquet Garni: Place 3 sprigs fresh parsley, ½ large bay leaf, and 1 sprig fresh thyme on a small square of clean cheesecloth. Pull cheesecloth up around herbs and tie closed with string to form a bundle.

Soupe à l'Oignon Gratinée
(French Onion Soup)

1 tablespoon butter
2 tablespoons olive oil
4 large onions, halved and
  thinly sliced
3 cloves garlic, minced
1 teaspoon sugar
½ teaspoon dried thyme
2 tablespoons all-purpose flour

8 cups beef broth
½ cup dry white wine
2 tablespoons cognac
  (optional)
6 to 8 thick slices French
  bread, toasted (below)
about 2 cups freshly
  grated Swiss cheese

In large, heavy saucepan, melt butter with olive oil over
medium high heat. Add onions. Sauté 10 minutes, or until softened and beginning to brown. Reduce heat to medium. Add
garlic, sugar, and thyme. Cook 30 more minutes, or until onions
are browned well, stirring frequently. Stir in flour, blending well.
Add beef broth and wine. Bring to boil. Skim off and discard
any foam on surface. Reduce heat and simmer 45 minutes, stirring occasionally. Remove from heat. Stir in cognac, if desired.
Arrange 6 to 8 ovenproof soup crocks on large baking sheet. Fill
about ¾ full with soup. Float toast on top. Sprinkle with Swiss
cheese. Broil a few inches from heat 3 to 4 minutes, or just until
cheese melts. Serve immediately. Makes 6 to 8 servings.

Toasted French Bread: Arrange slices in single layer on baking
sheet. Bake at 325 degrees for 15 minutes. Lightly brush both
sides with olive oil. Bake additional 15 minutes, or until dry and
lightly browned. Rub tops with cut garlic.

Soufflé au Fromage
(Cheese Soufflé)

1 teaspoon butter, softened
1 tablespoon freshly grated
   Parmesan cheese
3 tablespoons butter
3 tablespoons all-purpose flour
1 cup boiling milk
½ teaspoon salt
⅛ teaspoon coarsely ground
   black pepper
dash of cayenne (red pepper)

dash of nutmeg
4 egg yolks
5 egg whites,
   room temperature
dash of salt
½ cup freshly grated
   Swiss cheese
¼ cup freshly grated
   Parmesan cheese
additional grated cheese

Butter 6-cup soufflé dish with softened butter. Sprinkle with 1 tablespoon grated Parmesan cheese, turning dish to coat bottom and side. Set aside. In medium saucepan, melt 3 tablespoons butter over medium heat. Whisk in flour. Cook and whisk 2 minutes or until foamy. Remove from heat. When foam subsides, add boiling milk all at once. Whisk until blended well. Add ½ teaspoon salt, pepper, cayenne, and nutmeg. Return to medium heat. Bring to boil, whisking constantly. Boil and whisk 1 minute. (Mixture should be very thick.) Remove from heat. Add egg yolks one at a time, whisking to blend well after each addition. Remove from heat and set aside. In clean bowl, place egg whites and dash of salt. Beat until stiff but not dry and peaks form. Fold about a fourth of the egg whites into the cooked egg yolk mixture. Stir in Swiss and Parmesan cheeses. Gently fold in remaining egg whites. Spoon mixture into prepared soufflé dish. Carefully smooth top. Sprinkle with additional grated cheese. Place on middle rack of preheated 400-degree oven. Immediately reduce oven to 375 degrees. Bake 30 minutes or until puffy and golden brown. Serve immediately (do not let stand). Makes 4 to 6 servings.

Oeufs à la Neige
(Snowy Eggs or Floating Islands)

8 egg yolks
¼ cup sugar
2½ cups scalded milk
1 teaspoon vanilla extract

4 egg whites,
   room temperature
¼ teaspoon cream of tartar
1¼ cups superfine sugar
ground nutmeg

In medium saucepan, whisk egg yolks and sugar until thick and creamy. Gradually add scalded milk, whisking constantly. Stir constantly over medium heat until sauce thickens enough to coat back of spoon. (Do not boil.) Transfer to bowl. Stir in vanilla extract. Cool to room temperature. Cover and refrigerate until chilled. Half fill a large skillet or saucepan with water. Bring to a gentle simmer. (Do not boil.) Meanwhile, beat egg whites and cream of tartar until foamy. Add superfine sugar, 2 tablespoons at a time, beating until stiff and glossy. Spoon heaping tablespoonfuls of meringue (about the size and shape of small eggs) into simmering water, a few at a time. Poach 2 to 3 minutes or just until firm, turning once. Using slotted spoon, transfer to paper-towel-lined baking sheet to drain. Pour chilled custard into individual serving dishes. Arrange meringues on top. Sprinkle with nutmeg. Serve immediately. Makes 4 to 6 servings.

Ask just about anyone, anywhere, anytime to name the French restaurant of choice, and Le Bec-Fin will glide off the tongue without hesitation. I had heard about Le Bec-Fin from a family friend several years ago and knew this upscale Philadelphia restaurant deserved more than a glance in any chapter devoted to French cuisine.

Le Bec-Fin has a global reputation for perfecting culinary masterpieces under the day-to-day, hands-on scrutiny of chef and owner Georges Perrier. In fact, Le Bec-Fin has been described more than once as the best French restaurant in the country, maybe the world, and Philadelphia Mayor Ed Rendell named the street in front of the restaurant after Perrier.

Why all the fuss? Because Perrier is a marvel at developing innovative nouvelle cuisine and seems never to run out of creative recipe ideas. There's Cailles Farcies au Cresson, Galette de Crabe, Le Bec-Fin, and Eventail d'Agneau au Romar, all superlative entrées, followed by fine cheeses and Perrier's own fruit and nut bread presented on a magnificent silver serving cart. A second, triple-tiered cart holds more than forty desserts made daily in the Le Bec-Fin bakery and includes rich specialties like Soufflé Glace au Grand Marnier and Gâteau le Bec-Fin. You can also choose from an extensive list of wines and liquors.

Although Perrier serves dishes rich in calories and fat, the menu has evolved from classical French to nouvelle cuisine in an effort to lighten up and please health-conscious patrons. About these changes, Perrier says, "In 1970, our beurre blanc sauce was a wonderfully lavish reduction of large amounts of butter and cream. Today, I think it would be impossibly rich and very few people would include it in their diet. Everyone wants wonderful taste, but they want it lighter. That is difficult to do. We find better combinations of ingredients and better techniques. We blow air into some of the sauces to make them lighter, but we never forget that, as always, our patrons deserve the best and the freshest ingredients prepared *à le bec-fin*—to the good taste."

Perrier, himself, visits the dining room often to check on the quality of his restaurant's service and cuisine. He's quite dramatic at times, sabering bottles of Dom Pérignon for a demanding lunch crowd, then bowing to loud applause before heading back to the kitchen. He just wrote his first cookbook, called *Perrier's Le Bec-Fin Cookbook* (Running Press, 1997).

Rejecting invitations to relocate in Manhattan, Chicago, and Los Angeles, Perrier moved his Philadelphia restaurant to a historic art deco building in Center City a few years back and created what has been described as the most elegant dining atmosphere in the country. You'll find French period furniture, mantled fireplaces, crystal chandeliers, brilliant mirrors, and exotic fresh flower arrangements.

Le Bec-Fin is located at 1523 Walnut St. in Philadelphia. Dinner is served Monday through Saturday, with early and late seatings daily, prix fixe $102. Lunch is also served with seatings Monday through Friday. Reservations are required for lunch and dinner. Valet parking is available. For reservations or more information, call (215) 567-1000.

TWELFTH NIGHT

In many countries, Twelfth Night marks the end of the Christmas season. In the church, however, Twelfth Night symbolizes the beginning of Epiphany, or the day Jesus was shown to the wise men who had followed the star. Often called kings, the wise men brought expensive gifts such as gold, frankincense, and myrrh to Jesus.

In thirteenth-century France, the monks of Mont-Saint-Michel celebrated Twelfth Night with a party and cake called Gâteau des Rois. A dry bean was placed in the cake. The man or woman who found the bean was "crowned" king or queen of the celebration and chose a partner to reign with him or her for the night. Each of the remaining partygoers drew fictitious names from a dish and were to act like that character for the rest of the evening.

During the Christmas season in France, you will still see the Gâteau des Rois topped with three kings to symbolize the wise men of Twelfth Night. You can make your own cake and top it with cutout kings or even small toy crowns. Here is one of many recipes for Gâteau des Rois.

Gâteau de Rois
(Lemon Sponge Cake)

8 egg yolks
¼ cup water
1 tablespoon fresh lemon juice
1 teaspoon freshly grated
    lemon peel
1 teaspoon vanilla extract

1½ cups sugar, divided
¾ teaspoon salt
1½ cups all-purpose flour
8 egg whites
1 teaspoon cream of tartar
lemon frosting (below)

In medium bowl, beat egg yolks on high speed 6 minutes or until thick. In separate bowl, combine water, lemon juice, lemon peel, and vanilla extract. Add to egg yolks, blending on low speed. Gradually add the salt and ¾ cup of the sugar, beating until sugar dissolves. Sprinkle ¼ cup of the flour over the egg yolk mixture. Gently fold in with rubber spatula. Fold in remaining flour, ¼ cup at a time. Set aside. In large, clean bowl, and using clean beaters, beat egg whites with cream of tartar on medium speed 1 minute or until soft peaks form. Gradually add remaining ¾ cup sugar, 1 tablespoon at a time, beating until stiff peaks form. Stir about 1 cup of the egg whites into the egg yolk mixture. Fold all of the egg yolk mixture into remaining egg whites, blending well. Spoon into ungreased 10-inch tube pan. Bake at 325 degrees for 1 hour, or until cake springs back when lightly touched. Cool completely upside down in pan. Run metal spatula or knife around side of pan to loosen cake. Remove from pan and lightly frost or glaze with lemon frosting. Makes 10 to 12 servings.

Lemon Frosting: In large bowl, blend 2 cups unsifted confectioner's sugar and ¼ cup softened butter. Beat in 1 tablespoon light cream and freshly grated peel and juice of 1 lemon. Add small amount additional light cream as needed for desired consistency.

Germany

Heartland Paths to Follow

William Penn, a Quaker, founded Pennsylvania with a written provision for religious freedom for all. When Penn visited Germany during the 1670s touting religious freedom in the colonies, he gained an impressive following among religious dissenters there as well.

The German Mennonites were the first to settle in Pennsylvania. On October 6, 1683, thirteen Mennonite families sailed from Germany on the *Concord* and landed in Philadelphia, the primary port of arrival for early immigrants. They founded nearby Germantown, where they faced religious persecution, prejudice, and starvation. Other German religious groups, including the Cloisters, Brethren, Amish, Lutherans, and Catholics, followed the lead of the Mennonites and migrated to Pennsylvania. Discouraged by oppression, however, many of these German settlers pressed west to present-day Lancaster County, where they welcomed the isolation, freedom, and challenges of starting from scratch.

Lancaster County remains synonymous with the Pennsylvania Dutch, a catchphrase for various groups of German settlers. Some claim that the term *Dutch* originated with English settlers who confused German and Swiss languages with that spoken by the Dutch. Others say the German word *Deutsch*, which means German, was simply distorted to *Dutch*.

The fiercely independent "Dutch" reluctantly learned English so they could communicate and do business with their neighbors but maintained a form of Low German that blended English and German into a language all its own. We still hear Amish phrases like "spritz the grass" and "outen the light," examples of Pennsylvania Dutch lingo.

Exploring Pennsylvania's German food heritage seems like an endless journey. Bread and starchy foods such as noodles, dumplings, and mush form the basis for many German meals, because in the "old days," flour was an inexpensive and readily available ingredient.

Sauerkraut was finely cut cabbage fermented in its own juices to serve as a side dish with beef, pork, and veal sausages. Tzitterly-souse, or pickled pigs' feet, was a popular dish, as was tzeibach-sweiback, or twice-baked bread. Homemade yeast called satz was actually a starter made from a small amount of batter from the last batch of bread.

You can travel to just about any county in Pennsylvania to learn about German culture; examine handmade German quilts, sturdy furniture, and colorful art; and sample extremely satisfying food. Most counties hold some kind of German folk festival or Dutch Days, with traditional food, music, and wares. There are hundreds of traditional German recipes and just as many restaurants to prepare them here in Pennsylvania.

The Shady Maple Smorgasbord in East Earl, about a mile east of Blue Ball on Route 23, is characteristic of many traditional Pennsylvania Dutch restaurants—quaint, family oriented, and inviting to those who want a casual, filling meal. For about $12, you can choose from a buffet table of homemade specialties such as baked ham, meat loaf with brown gravy, and roast chicken, and then move on to a clean, large, cafeterialike dining area. Efficient waitresses wearing crisply ruffled caps and aprons take away your emptied plates and invite you to go for seconds, thirds, as much as you can handle. Shady Maple is open Monday through Saturday for breakfast, lunch, and dinner.

The Lehigh Valley Mall in Whitehall is a less likely spot for a German restaurant, but Bill Baker, owner of the mall's Dunderbak's Restaurant, has done a good job of merging the ways of the "old country" with the food preferences of the credit-card-toting American shopper.

Dunderbak's offers Bavarian-American cuisine, as well as an excellent selection of German beer. The restaurant proudly touts itself as the only authorized "Spaten Brauhaus" in Pennsylvania, featuring four drafts from the Spaten Brewery in Munich, Germany. Most beers run $2.50 a mug up to $6 for a hofbrau liter. You can also buy six-packs of imported beer and customized, gourmet gift baskets in the little gift shop that is an integral part of Dunderbak's. The gourmet foods, cookware, and German smokers are beautiful and offer a nice change of pace to shoppers who want something different.

Dunderbak's does have deli sandwiches, pitas, and traditional American-style dinners, but the Bavarian dishes make the menu. There are plenty of German sausage varieties, various side dishes such as hot potato salad and Dutch potato filling, and scrumptious desserts such as German chocolate cake and apple dumplings.

Dunderbak's is open during normal mall hours and then some. Call (610) 264-4963 for specific hours, dinner specials, and gift orders.

Mid-June was downright hot when I visited a flurry of food events in Lancaster County. My first stop was the Route 340 Pennsylvania Dutch Food and Folk Fair in the town of Bird in Hand. The fair was in its third year, a small but mighty festival drawing about 5,000 and benefitting the Lancaster County Food Bank.

My son, Michael, darted off to pet an assortment of nicely groomed goats and Belgian horses while I went to the food tent. Eight local restaurateurs served up Pennsylvania Dutch classics like chicken pot pie, chicken corn soup, pork and sauerkraut, meat loaf, and shoo-fly pie. Kitchen Kettle Village offered snitz and knepp, a hearty combination of chopped ham, cooked dried apples, and potato dumplings served with grilled ham slices on the side. At the Stoltzfus Farm Restaurant booth, I had mildly seasoned sausage tucked in a soft roll and heaped with sautéed onions, chopped green pepper, and a not-too-spicy tomato sauce. Prices were very reasonable, and the two of us enjoyed all of our food for less than $10.

Each hour during the Route 340 Fair, culinary experts show traditional preparation techniques for classic German foods like sausage, sticky buns, pot pie, and apple dumplings. There also are plenty of local artisans making pottery, baskets, candles, braided rugs, wood carvings, brooms, and of course, quilts. Warning: Although there is no admission charge for the fair, plan to take some cash along for the food and the one-of-a-kind crafts. You'll be tempted to buy.

After the fair, you should make time for some of Bird in Hand's "touristy" businesses, like the farmers' market right across the street. The gourmet foods and crafts make wonderful gifts for friends and family across the country, who probably know about the Pennsylvania Dutch and groups like the Amish but don't have the opportunity to enjoy this form of German culture firsthand.

The Route 340 Pennsylvania Dutch Food and Folk Fair is held the third weekend in June. Admission and parking are free. Call (717) 768-8272 for more information.

After lunch at the fair, Michael and I moved on to the Artworks Expo Center in Ephrata for the Food, Farm and Fun Fest—as if we needed anything else to eat. This event had a more commercial flavor than the Route 340 Fair. Regional businesses—Doneckers, Pennfield Farms, The Rose 101.3 FM, Seltzer's, and the Penn-Dutch Traveler—sponsor the Ephrata festival and describe their event as "the best of Lancaster County's plentiful foods, from farm to your table." More than forty Lancaster County food businesses exhibit everything from honey to organic produce and hand out free samples to some 15,000 visitors, and the adjacent four-story Artworks mall houses several artists' galleries, showcasing fine art, beautifully crafted jewelry, collectibles, and designer quilts.

Before I left the fest, I tried to say hello to Betty Groff, nationally known Lancaster County restaurateur, cookbook author, and successful entrepreneur best known for Groff's Farm, her Pennsylvania Dutch restaurant in Mount Joy. She also owns and operates the more upscale Cameron Estate Inn and Restaurant about 4 miles from the Farm. Betty is a regional celebrity with an impressive following, however, and the huge crowd around her table kept me at a distance. I did manage to grab a free copy of the winning recipes from her Most Delightful Dessert Contest just held at the fest.

Another contest at the fest was Pennfield Farms' Chicken Recipe Cook-Off, which would be held the following day. Area cooks would prepare their favorite chicken dishes, hoping to win the $1,000 grand prize. Samples of the various dishes would be available to the public after the judging.

Lancaster County's Food, Farm and Fun Fest is located at the Art-works Expo Center at 100 N. State St. in Ephrata. Admission is $2 per adult and free for children under 12. There's plenty of free parking. Hours run noon to 5 P.M. on Friday and 10 A.M. to 5 P.M. on Saturday. For more information, call (717) 738-9500.

The Food, Farm and Fun Fest and the Route 340 Fair are two of several events promoted each June by the Pennsylvania Dutch Convention and Visitors Bureau as a way to showcase the area's cuisine. You can spend that same weekend in the Lancaster area enjoying activities like a progressive dinner and narrated twilight walking tour of downtown Lancaster, a "hands-on" Amish cooking class, an apple fritter demonstration at the Historic Strasburg Inn, or a tour of Lancaster's historic Central Market, one of the nation's oldest farmers' markets.

There were plenty of food demonstrations that June weekend. The German toy candy presentation at the Cake and Candy Emporium on Route 72 was probably the most interesting. Toy candy is clear and colored vibrant red, yellow, or green, but unlike most hard candies, it is not flavored. It requires just three ingredients—water, sugar, and corn syrup—and, as a result, reflects the simplicity of the Pennsylvania Germans, who began making the candy in the mid-1800s.

Two Philadelphia foundries, Thomas Mills Brothers and V. Clad Company, made 420 molds in a wide variety of shapes, sizes, and styles to accommodate the candy as it hardened. Pennsylvania German children would find the toy-shaped candy in their Christmas stockings. Small boys and girls enjoyed clear toy candy trains and animals and served imaginary tea in clear candy cups, saucers, pitchers, and baskets.

If you're into cookbooks and want to collect some excellent German recipes, be sure to take some time during your Pennsylvania Dutch food weekend to stop at the Mennonite Information Center at 2209 Millstream Rd. in Lancaster. You can get a 10 to 15 percent discount on your cookbook purchases, and the Center has more than fifty to pore over. I chose *Treasured Mennonite Recipes*, vol. 1 (Fox Chapel Publishing, 1992), an authentic collection pulled together by Mennonite Relief Sale Volunteers. (Relief sales are organized by local volunteers from the Mennonite and Brethren in Christ Churches to raise money for third-world development projects.) This 220-page cookbook describes the Mennonites and gives an interesting history about their relief sale efforts. The recipes are easy to follow and give wonderful results.

You can get more information on the various Pennsylvania Dutch food events held each June in the Lancaster area, as well as a free map and visitors guide, by calling the Pennsylvania Dutch Convention and Visitors Bureau at (800) 723-8824, ext. 2425.

Chicken Rivel Soup

8 cups chicken broth
2 cups all-purpose flour
1 teaspoon salt
dash white pepper
2 eggs, slightly beaten
2 cups frozen whole-kernel
   corn, thawed

1 medium onion, chopped
2 tablespoons snipped
   fresh parsley
2 cups diced cooked
   chicken

In large saucepan, bring chicken broth to full boil. Meanwhile, in large bowl combine flour, salt, pepper, and eggs, mixing well. Gradually drop small clumps of flour mixture ("rivels") into boiling broth, stirring constantly. Reduce heat. Add corn, onion, and parsley. Cover and simmer 10 minutes, stirring occasionally. Add chicken. Heat through. Makes 6 to 8 servings.

Chicken Pot Pie

4- to 5-pound stewing chicken
canned chicken broth, as needed
4 medium potatoes, peeled
  and chopped
2 tablespoons snipped
  fresh parsley

salt and pepper, to taste
1½ cups all-purpose flour
½ teaspoon salt
2 eggs, slightly beaten
3 tablespoons light cream

Place chicken in large kettle or Dutch oven and cover with water. Cover and bring to boil. Reduce heat and simmer, covered, 2 hours, or until meat is tender and cooked through. Remove chicken from cooking water and set aside to cool slightly. Adjust cooking water to equal 4 cups, adding canned chicken broth as needed. Stir in potatoes, parsley, salt, and pepper. Cover broth and keep warm over low heat. Remove skin and bones from chicken, chop meat, and set aside. In medium bowl, combine flour and ½ teaspoon salt. Make well in center. Add eggs and cream. Stir until soft dough forms. Transfer to lightly floured surface. Using floured rolling pin, roll thin. Cut into 2- to 3-inch squares to form pot pie dough. Bring broth mixture to boil. Carefully drop pot pie squares onto surface of broth so that they lay flat. Reduce heat to medium. Cover and cook 30 minutes. Add chicken. Makes 6 to 8 servings.

The Kutztown Folk Festival is almost fifty years old now and is probably the best-known Pennsylvania Dutch festival. The event recently moved to the Schuylkill County Fairgrounds in Summit Station to make more room for the dozens of exhibits, vendors, and demonstrations. There's a nineteenth-century village, a museum of antique farm machinery, a nature center, and plenty of farm animals to pet. Barns and tents full of crafts and foods should keep you busy, even in bad weather.

I found lots of specialty Pennsylvania Dutch foods—pickles, dried apples, and jellies—to take home. The warm soft pretzels, funnel cake, and sausage were best eaten on the spot, and there were generous wedges of shoo-fly pie to eat there or take home.

The Kutztown Folk Festival runs from the end of June through the first week of July, 10 A.M. to 8 P.M. daily. Admission is $10 for adults and

$5 for children age 12 and under. Children under 5 get in free. For more information, write to Festival Associates, 461 Vine Lane, Kutztown, PA 19530, or call (610) 683-8707.

Funnel Cakes

2 cups all-purpose flour
1 teaspoon baking powder
½ teaspoon salt
1½ cups milk

2 eggs, slightly beaten
vegetable oil
sifted confectioner's sugar

In large bowl, combine flour, baking powder, and salt. Stir in milk and eggs. In deep fat fryer or skillet, heat about 2 inches of oil to 375 degrees. Holding bottom of a funnel closed with a finger, pour some of the batter into the funnel. Release finger from bottom of funnel, allowing batter to flow in a circular motion, then in a crisscross pattern, into the hot oil. Cook just until lightly browned. Remove from oil and drain on paper towels. Repeat frying until all batter is used. Sprinkle with confectioner's sugar. Serve hot. Makes about 1 dozen.

Shoo-Fly Pie

The Pennsylvania Dutch may be best known for their shoo-fly pie, rich layers of molasses filling and sugary crumbs baked in a traditional pastry shell. There are two theories on the origin of the pie's name. Some believe that the 1800s Amish women baked the pie from readily available ingredients such as flour, water, molasses, and shortening. Once baked, the pies were placed on open windowsills to cool and thus attracted flies, which had to be constantly shooed away. The second theory rests with the brand name Shoofly Molasses, which was used by the Pennsylvania Germans in their desserts during the mid-1800s.

1 cup all-purpose flour	¾ cup hot water
⅔ cup packed brown sugar	1 cup molasses
1 tablespoon shortening	1 egg, slightly beaten
1 teaspoon baking soda	9-inch unbaked pie shell

In large bowl, combine flour and brown sugar. Cut in shortening with pastry blender or fork until mixture forms coarse crumbs. Measure out and set aside ½ cup of the crumbs. In small bowl, dissolve baking soda in hot water. Add baking soda mixture, molasses, and egg to crumbs in bowl. Mix well and pour into unbaked pie shell. Sprinkle with reserved ½ cup crumbs. Bake at 375 degrees for 35 minutes, or until almost set. Cool completely before slicing. Makes 6 to 8 servings.

In September, you will want to return to the heart of Pennsylvania Dutch country to celebrate the end of the fall harvest at the Seven Sweets and Sours festival. Kitchen Kettle Village in Intercourse hosts this fun event to commemorate the German tradition of preserving the last of the autumn produce in a vinegar and sugar brine. You can watch as village workers cook and vacuum-pack a variety of sweet-and-sour dishes, including a zesty corn relish, sweet bell pepper relish, and chow-chow, in clear glass jars, and you can buy these delicious German dishes to take home.

Kitchen Kettle Village includes a number of small, quaint shops housing crafts, gifts, food, and samples to eat on the run. For more information on the village and Seven Sweets and Sours celebration, call (717) 768-8261.

Lebanon County devotes a three-day September weekend each year to lunch meat—Lebanon bologna, to be specific. Crowds browse the exhibition hall at the Lebanon Bologna Fest and sample their favorite smoked sausage, made by one of just six Pennsylvania-based companies, including the Daniel Weaver Company in Lebanon. Every brand of Lebanon bologna has its own unique flavor, but all are smoked and seasoned with herbs and spices, just as the German settlers made the summer sausage a century ago. At that time, beef was hung from rafters to ferment and dry according to various family recipes. This method of preservation allowed the Germans to store the meat for extended periods and pack it in their lunch boxes without spoiling.

Today, manufacturers blend ground beef with salt, sugar, and secret spice blends, then hang the product in 100-degree smokehouses for two to four days. The sausage is cured with liquid smoke or, for a more rustic approach, exposed to aged sawdust smoldering over hardwood logs. The meat's sweet, smoky flavor is recognized across the country.

The Lebanon Bologna Fest is held the first full weekend in September at the Lebanon Valley Expo and Fairground on Rocherty Road, just east of Route 72. It runs from 2 to 10 P.M. on Friday, 11 A.M. to 10 P.M. on Saturday, and 10 A.M. to 9 P.M. on Sunday. Admission is $4 for adults and $3 for children ages 4 to 12.

Across the state, Pittsburgh's Penn Brewery holds its annual Oktoberfest to celebrate German cuisine and beer during the last two weekends in September. Oktoberfest originated in Munich, Germany, in 1810 to celebrate the engagement of the Bavarian crown prince. The original fall festival lasted sixteen days and included massive quantities of beer and food. Today, hundreds squeeze into Penn's nineteenth-century brick brewing complex and don't seem to mind the lengthy food lines as they sip Oktoberfest Bier, made from an authentic Munich recipe. Twelve other beers are made there, too, all according to Germany's beer purity law of 1516, which permitted the use of just four ingredients: barley, hops, yeast, and water.

Penn Brewery is proud to be the home of Penn Pilsner and the first "Tied House" (brewery-owned restaurant) in Pennsylvania since prohibition. During Oktoberfest, you can enjoy a full German meal in the cozy, wood-paneled Rathskeller or eat a more casual meal outside on the open, upstairs patio. The Rathskeller was serving its full menu during the fest and offered every German food imaginable. Most entrees cost less than $12. On the patio upstairs, chefs were roasting a pig on an open-air grill and setting up a buffet near casual outdoor dining tables. Meanwhile, guests drank beer, listened to lively polka music, and talked with family and friends. The crowd was upbeat and didn't seem to mind the somewhat chaotic atmosphere. The patio menu was devoted to Oktoberfest and included casual fare.

All year round you can enjoy tours of Penn Brewery, described in the brochure as *Gemutlichkeit,* or "good food and good times." You'll learn how German beer is made and see a beautiful display of Penn's German-made copper brewing kettles. Owned and operated by the Pastorius family, the oldest German family in America, Penn Brewery is tucked away on a hill above Troy Hill Road just off Chestnut Street and near the H. J. Heinz catsup factory. The Penn Brewery Oktoberfest runs Friday, Saturday, and Sunday afternoons through evenings with no general admission. Parking is free but somewhat limited, with some shuttle service available. For more information, call (412) 237-9402.

Harmony, Pennsylvania, rests on the spot where major Indian trails converged to form an Indian village two centuries ago. Located in western Pennsylvania, Harmony was named after the Harmonists, a group of German religious followers who pledged all of their possessions to a self-proclaimed prophet called George Rapp. In the early 1800s, Rapp, then a vinetender, assembled his following in Germany and promised them religious freedom in the New World. They called themselves the Harmony Society and chose the self-sufficiency of a 2,000-acre settlement that included a church, school, tavern, gristmill, brewery, distillery, and tannery.

Harmony prospered until 1807, when the Society adopted celibacy as its platform, the first step toward the group's extinction. Shortly after, the Harmonists decided to start afresh and moved west to Indiana. The original town of Harmony was sold to German Mennonites and gradually began to prosper again.

Today, Historic Harmony, Inc., works to preserve the buildings and artifacts of the original settlement by sponsoring its annual Dankfest, now more than twenty-five years old. In addition to German music, dancing, crafts, and museum tours, you can enjoy lots of classic German foods—sausages with sauerkraut, potato salad, red cabbage slaw, fried green tomatoes, funnel cakes, and potato pancakes—prepared by village volunteers. Volunteers gather two weeks in advance of Dankfest to make root beer from scratch and fill the glass bottles carefully, since, according to one helper, the bottles tend to explode.

You can enjoy Dankfest the fourth weekend in August. It's held on Saturday and Sunday afternoons until 6:00 P.M., and proceeds benefit the Harmony Museum. Call (412) 452-7341 for more information on Dankfest and tours.

Warm Potato Salad

8 medium potatoes	1 cup sugar
8 hard-cooked eggs, diced	½ cup cider vinegar
1 cup chopped celery	2 tablespoons mayonnaise
1 cup chopped onion	2 teaspoons mustard
4 eggs, slightly beaten	salt and pepper, to taste

Cook potatoes in water until tender. Set aside to cool. Peel and dice. In large bowl toss diced potatoes with hard-cooked eggs, celery, and onion. In top of double boiler, combine eggs, sugar, and vinegar. Cook over hot (not boiling) water, stirring constantly, until mixture thickens. Remove from heat. Stir in mayonnaise and mustard, blending well. Toss warm dressing with potato mixture and salt and pepper to taste. Serve warm. Makes 10 to 12 servings.

Southern Somerset County provides a scenic autumn backdrop for the Springs German Folk Festival. Located in the heart of maple country (to quote the festival brochure), the mountain village of Springs lies near the Maryland border. Juried craftspeople spin, weave, braid, paint, and dip their wares for the public. You'll also see lots of antique farm equipment and home furnishings, as well as a blacksmith, tinsmith, and ropemaker.

Of course, there's plenty of food in the Pennsylvania-German tradition. You can enjoy a family-style German dinner of country sausage, Dutch-fried potatoes, and corn or eat from the various concessions serving freshly made doughnuts, funnel cakes, apple butter bread, and bean soup. After you're full, you can watch and learn how sauerkraut, bread, and maple syrup were made during the pioneer days.

For many years, Omar and Myra Maust were in charge of the festival's food and made sure thousands of festival visitors and some 250 workers were fed daily. In the early years of the festival, Myra would fry pound after pound of Dutch potatoes after local volunteers did the initial cooking in their homes. Nowadays, eight women peel, one slices, and three fry the potatoes after they are cooked in massive kettles right on the grounds. (Myra has retired from the position of fryer.)

Springs volunteers and area food vendors still use original, old-fashioned Dutch-German recipes to make such traditional food as applesauce, apple butter, fried corn mush, and bean soup for the festival. Yeast bread is made in an outdoor bake oven, and butter is freshly churned. Prices are very reasonable, and you'll want to take food home to enjoy later.

The Springs Folk Festival is located on Route 669 southwest of Salisbury and runs the first Friday and Saturday in October from 9 to 5 daily. Admission is $4 for adults and $1 for children. Call (814) 662-4158 or 662-2051 for information.

German Gingersnaps

1 cup sugar	2 teaspoons baking soda
¾ cup shortening	1 teaspoon ground ginger
¼ cup molasses	1 teaspoon cinnamon
1 egg	½ teaspoon cloves
2 cups all-purpose flour	¼ teaspoon salt

In large bowl, cream sugar, shortening, molasses, and egg. In separate bowl, combine 1 cup of the flour, baking soda, ginger, cinnamon, cloves, and salt. Stir into creamed mixture, blending well. Stir in remaining 1 cup flour. Drop by rounded teaspoonfuls onto lightly greased baking sheets. Bake at 350 degrees for 8 to 10 minutes, or until lightly browned. Cool slightly on baking sheets. Remove to wire racks and cool completely. Makes about 5 dozen.

I borrow many of my December decorating and food ideas from the Germans. After all, the Old World German Christmas is the basis for many of our American holiday traditions.

The Hershey Museum in "Chocolatetown, U.S.A." places strong emphasis on the Pennsylvania Dutch community and its history. As a part of this focus, the Museum re-creates a German Christkindlmarkt, or "Christ Child Market," during the first full weekend of each December. The market gives museum visitors an opportunity to shop for authentic German decorations, gifts, and food in a Currier and Ives atmosphere—my kind of Christmas shopping. The *Belsnickel* ("bringer of gifts") arrives at the market on Saturday wearing fur from head to foot to commemorate the rustic German villager who delivered gifts and candy to the good children of his community generations ago. (Apparently, the bad children were switched.) And the crafts vendors offer more than the usual mall assortment of gifts.

The food at Christkindlmarkt is more than tempting. Your choice of knockwurst (beef sausage) or bratwurst (pork and veal sausage) is served with sauerkraut, onions, and sweet bell peppers. If it's a cold day, you may go for the chicken corn soup, a classic and very filling Pennsylvania Dutch soup. Top it off with a slice of rich Black Forest cake, a dark chocolate cake with sweet cherries and thick cream, or a streusel made from soft pretzel dough. Apple dumplings, schnitz (dried apples) and soft pretzels are available, too, and fun to snack on while you listen to a German band and watch for the first flakes of holiday snow that go so well with an old-fashioned, Old World Christmas.

The Hershey Museum's Christkindlmarkt runs the first Friday, Saturday, and Sunday of December till 5 P.M. There is no admission, but tickets into the Hershey Museum for nonmembers cost $4.25 per adult and $2 for children. Parking around the museum costs $5. Call (717) 534-3439 for more information.

Historic downtown Bethlehem pays homage to its name and 1700s German architecture with its own version of Christkindlmarkt, patterned after the centuries-old Bavarian yuletide celebration. You'll find lots of German food, gifts, and entertainment at Bethlehem's Spring and Main Streets. Nutcrackers, ornaments, and Hummels are available, but many of the foods are perfect for gift giving, too. Roasted almonds, gourmet coffees, apricot rolls, poppy seed buns, gourmet soups, mustards, and fruit butters can be purchased at the event and taken home for friends and family.

If you get hungry at the Bethlehem fest, try an assortment of German foods offered in the Tannenbaum Cafe. You can enjoy a sizzling German pork and sauerkraut platter for less than $5, and they also have potato pancakes. Helmut's Strudel, from Glenshaw, has some wonderful German strudels, like apple, cherry, cheese, and apricot. If you aren't in the mood for something sweet, try Helmut's spinach and broccoli puffs or beef Wellington. Hatley Family Concessions serves a nonalcoholic version of Germany's steaming, spiced wine called Gluwein. I highly recommend it as a cure for Christmas chills and weary bones.

Bethlehem's Christkindlmarkt attracts more than 15,000 visitors and benefits the community arts fund. Admission is $4 per adult, and children enter free. A $6 unlimited entry pass is also available at the door or in advance; it grants the user access throughout the duration of the event. Municipal parking is available, and "Holly the Trolley" pro-vides transportation to and from the various parking areas. The event runs Thursdays through Sundays between Thanksgiving and Christmas, 11 A.M. to 7 P.M. Call (610) 861-0678 for information.

FASTNACHT DAY

The Pennsylvania Dutch prepare Fastnachts, rich yeast doughnuts without holes, for Shrove Tuesday, or Fastnacht Day. Tradition allows the consumption of these filling cakes the day before Ash Wednesday, the beginning of Lent—forty days of prayer, penance, and sacrifice, which included fasting.

In the old days, Germans made Fastnachts as a way to use up any remaining eggs and cream, since these ingredients would spoil before the end of Lent at Easter. They would eat the Fastnachts as sort of a last fling before the fasting began.

Fastnachts

1 package active dry yeast
¼ cup warm (not hot) water
¾ cup scalded milk, cooled
  to lukewarm
¼ cup sugar
¼ cup shortening

1 teaspoon salt
1 egg
3½ to 3¾ cups
  all-purpose flour
vegetable oil
sifted confectioner's sugar

In large bowl, dissolve yeast in warm water. Stir in milk, sugar, shortening, salt, and egg, blending well. Add 2 cups of the flour, blending well. Gradually add enough additional flour to form soft, but not sticky, dough. Turn onto lightly floured surface. Knead 5 minutes, or until smooth and elastic. Place in greased bowl, turning dough to lightly grease surface. Cover with damp cloth and let rise in warm place 1½ hours, or until doubled in volume. Punch down dough. Cover and let rise 30 more minutes, or until doubled again. Roll out onto lightly floured surface to ⅜ inch thickness. Cut with lightly floured doughnut cutter. Let rise, uncovered, on floured surface 30 minutes or until doubled and light. In large kettle or deep fat fryer, heat 3 to 4 inches of oil to 375 degrees. Drop doughnuts into hot fat a few at a time, turning as they rise to the surface. Fry 2 to 3 minutes, or until lightly browned. Remove from fat and drain on paper towels. Dust with confectioner's sugar while warm. Dust again when cooled. Makes about 2 dozen.

Poland

Kielbasa, Kapusta, and Where to Find Them

The Polish people have lived in America since colonial times, and of the thirteen colonies, Pennsylvania was home to the largest number. Until the 1870s, however, Poles made up one of the smaller ethnic groups in the commonwealth. Then, toward the end of the nineteenth century, Polish immigrants were drawn to Pennsylvania's industrial towns, especially within the northeastern coal-mining region of the state. Coal company advertisements promised a booming coal-mining industry, and the Poles, seeking to escape political and economic hardships at home, headed for the Wyoming Valley to find work.

The Polish newcomers were anxious to earn a living in the mines and, as a result, settled on below-standard wages. Miners who made more resented the Poles' willingness to work for less money. This attitude, coupled with language and cultural barriers, fostered resentment and difficulties for the hard-working Polish immigrants.

Many of the Poles began attending night school. After long, exhausting days in the mines, the new immigrants would learn the English language and American customs, hoping to open new doors and ease the transition from home. Soon, many Poles became craftsmen, tradesmen, butchers, carpenters, and tavern owners, no longer relying on the mines to earn meager wages. Their quality of life was improving, and sizable communities were thriving.

Polish-Americans love their food, probably more than any other culture, except maybe the French. Recipes from the "old country" have lasted through generations and evolved to blend with contemporary food trends in the United States. Today, meat, especially products such as the garlic-flavored sausage called kielbasa, is a more important part of the Polish diet than it was generations ago when meat was more scarce. In the old days, vegetables, grains, and fish took precedence over meat. Cabbage, used in recipes like sauerkraut and cabbage rolls, was grown in most Polish gardens, as were potatoes, beets, and barley. Grains were milled into flour for dark breads, and freshly caught pike or carp were cooked for evening meals.

Foreign influences often made a large impression on Polish cooks. Take, for example, visits from sixteenth-century Italian royalty. When Italy's dignitaries visited Poland, they insisted on taking their chefs along to ensure daily presentations of classic Italian cuisine. (It seems some Italians considered the Polish kitchen to be a haven for barbarians and a bit too rudimentary for their discerning tastes.) The Poles, not to be outdone, began to integrate Italian cooking methods and utilize "new" ingredients like tomatoes in the kitchen. In fact, to this day, Poles refer to vegetables as *wloszczyzna*—Italian produce.

Polish peasants also took great pride in their culinary skills and often relied on wild berries and mushrooms to help feed their families. Children learned the difference between a poisonous plant and one that would mean a deliciously prepared dinner that night. Vegetable soups and stews, buckwheat groats (kasza), and noodles were common and often topped with dollops of homemade sour cream.

Decades of Polish recipes are still in circulation and even offer insights into the Old World lifestyles of some Poles. *Uniwersalna Ksiazka Kucharska* (*The Universal Cookbook*) is considered the "bible" of Polish cooking. The book was first published around the end of the nineteenth century, although no one knows for sure. The author, Marja Ochorowicz-Monatowa, stated that the purpose of her book was to "give brides a knowledge of how cooking is done so that they may supervise the servants properly."

If you want to try some authentic Polish recipes, I recommend that you buy *Polish Cookery* (Crown Publishers, Inc., 1958). This Americanized version of *The Universal Cookbook* is translated and adapted by Jean Karsavina. The book's classic recipes are easy to read and call for readily available ingredients.

Traditionally, Poland has been predominantly Catholic, and many of the country's celebrations are held at churches. In the United States, Polish-Americans hold one of the country's largest and best-known Polish festivals at the national shrine of Our Lady of Czestochowa, near Doylestown. The massive Polish Catholic church holds almost 2,000 people, and up to a half million make pilgrimages to the shrine throughout the year.

On the warm August Sunday I visited the shrine to attend the Polish-American festival, the pews were filled to capacity, with little room left for standing. I pressed inside to see hundreds celebrating their religious beliefs against a backdrop of stained glass, original works of art, and pipe organ music. Most of the festival exhibits were outside, housed under tents or on tables. I saw plenty of beautiful, handmade items that looked more generic than ethnic, but there were also thoughtfully crafted Polish linens, delicate porcelain plates, and picture books designed to educate the youngest generation about their heritage.

Visitors were elbow-to-elbow as they moved from one display to the next, but they didn't seem to mind. After all, most were of Polish descent and there to better understand their culture. Although not Polish, I also wanted to learn more and found the perfect opportunity in Suzanne Strempek Shea.

Suzanne Shea is a Polish writer, a very good writer who has gained quite a following, not only within the Polish community, but among readers everywhere who enjoy good fiction. Shea writes charming, slice-of-life stories about Polish-American life.

Shea was at Doylestown's Polish Festival promoting her latest book, *Hoopi Shoopi Donna* (Pocket Books, 1996), the heartfelt story of a Polish-American father-daughter relationship. In the book, Shea details fabulous Polish meals. It was clear that Shea had grown up on authentic Polish meals, so I asked her to contribute one of her favorite family recipes to this book. Shea very graciously submitted the following version of those delicious little pasta pockets.

Pierogi

3 cups all-purpose flour	½ teaspoon salt
2 eggs, beaten	cabbage filling (below)
1 cup sour cream	melted butter

In large bowl, combine flour, eggs, sour cream, and salt. Let stand 20 minutes. Divide dough in half. Using floured rolling pin, roll dough out thin on lightly floured surface. Cut into circles using biscuit cutter. Place small spoonful of filling a little to one side on each round of dough. Moisten edge with water. Fold over and press edges together to seal shut. (Be sure to seal edges completely to keep filling from running out.) Drop pierogi, a few at a time, into boiling water. Cook gently 3 to 5 minutes after they float to the top. Using slotted spoon, carefully remove from water. Serve hot with melted butter. Makes 6 to 8 servings.

Cabbage Filling: Quarter 1 small head of cabbage. Cook in boiling, salted water 15 minutes. Drain, cool, and chop fine. In large skillet, melt 1 tablespoon butter. Add 1 finely chopped small onion and sauté 3 to 5 minutes. Add cabbage. Salt and pepper to taste. Sauté a few minutes to heat through and blend flavors. Cool completely before stuffing pierogi.

Doylestown's Polish-American Festival offered about 2 acres' worth of Polish food vendors mingled with carnival rides, games of chance, polka bands, and dancing. There was plenty of kielbasa—platters with sauerkraut, sandwiches, and the like. The kanapka, or ham and beef hoagies, were in demand that day, as were the potato placki, which were topped with sour cream or applesauce just before serving. There were plenty of hand-shaped pierogi and slices of babka, a sweet almond cake, and I saw people munching on them as they browsed and visited with old friends. The food was inexpensive, starting at 50 cents for a slice of babka to $3.25 for a generous kielbasa platter.

The Polish-American Festival is held each Labor Day weekend and the following weekend at the shrine located on Ferry Road just outside Doylestown. A $5 admission fee covers most activities, but food costs extra. Proceeds go to the national shrine. For more information, call (215) 345-0600.

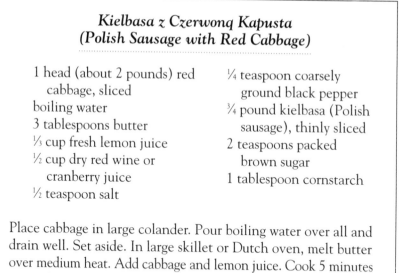

Kielbasa z Czerwonq Kapusta
(Polish Sausage with Red Cabbage)

1 head (about 2 pounds) red
   cabbage, sliced
boiling water
3 tablespoons butter
⅓ cup fresh lemon juice
½ cup dry red wine or
   cranberry juice
½ teaspoon salt

¼ teaspoon coarsely
   ground black pepper
¾ pound kielbasa (Polish
   sausage), thinly sliced
2 teaspoons packed
   brown sugar
1 tablespoon cornstarch

Place cabbage in large colander. Pour boiling water over all and drain well. Set aside. In large skillet or Dutch oven, melt butter over medium heat. Add cabbage and lemon juice. Cook 5 minutes or until cabbage turns pink, stirring constantly. Add wine or cranberry juice, salt, and pepper. Reduce heat to medium low. Cover and cook 45 minutes. In small bowl, thoroughly combine brown sugar and cornstarch. Whisk into cabbage mixture, blending well. Increase heat and bring mixture to a boil, whisking constantly. Reduce heat. Add sausage. Cover and simmer 30 minutes, or until sausage is completely cooked. Makes 4 servings.

Potato Placki (Potato Pancakes)

4 medium potatoes, peeled
  and grated
¼ cup all-purpose flour
4 eggs, well beaten
1 teaspoon salt

dash white pepper
vegetable oil
  cooking spray
applesauce or sour cream

In large bowl, combine potatoes, flour, eggs, salt, and pepper. Lightly coat a large skillet with cooking spray. Heat over medium heat. Spoon generous tablespoonfuls of potato mixture into hot skillet. Fry until bottoms are browned. Turn and continue frying until other sides are browned. Serve hot with applesauce or sour cream. Makes 6 to 8 servings.

There are few Pennsylvania restaurants that offer strictly Polish cuisine. Most establishments that come close are actually Eastern European in nature and may include foods from Russia, Ukraine, and Germany. The foods of these countries, although regionally varied, are similar in style to those of Poland.

Take Philadelphia's popular Warsaw Cafe, for example. Owner Marion Jarzemski describes his restaurant-bar as romantic, intimate, and Russian as much as it is Polish. The menu includes quite an impressive selection of Eastern European ethnic dishes, including some from Poland. There's an excellent borscht (that zesty beet soup), a tasty bigos (hunter's stew), and pierogi. The menu also lists several German, Russian, and Ukrainian dishes. Dinner prices range from about $13 to $18. The Warsaw Cafe is located at 306 S. 16th St. in Philadelphia and is open Monday through Saturday for lunch and dinner. Call (215) 546-0204 for reservations.

Bigos (Hunter's Stew)

1 pound ground beef
1 pound ground lamb
1 pound ground pork
2 slices thick bacon,
   cut into strips
½ medium onion, chopped
1 leek, minced
1 tablespoon all-purpose flour

2 cups sliced fresh
   mushrooms
1 cup beef bouillon
2 pounds sauerkraut,
   rinsed and drained well
1 teaspoon sugar
salt and coarsely ground
   black pepper, to taste
½ cup dry white wine

In large skillet, brown beef, lamb, and pork. Drain and discard excess liquid. Set meat aside. In large kettle or Dutch oven, fry bacon over medium heat. Drain and discard excess fat. Add onion and leek. Sauté 3 minutes. Stir in flour, blending well. Add mushrooms and bouillon. Bring to boil. Reduce heat and simmer 5 minutes. Stir in sauerkraut, sugar, and browned meat. Salt and pepper to taste. Cover and simmer over medium low heat 1½ hours. Add wine. Gently simmer 15 minutes. (Do not boil.) Makes 6 to 8 servings.

THE POLISH EASTER

Easter is the most important holiday in Poland and one of the happiest days of the year. Poles observe forty days of fasting during Lent, and when Easter finally arrives, families are anxious for a feast.

The Poles observe Easter with traditions much like those of Ukraine. On Good Friday eve, hard-cooked eggs are colored and elaborately decorated. On Easter Sunday, baskets are filled to the top with salt, hard-cooked eggs, butter, and other foods, then carried to church to be blessed by the priest.

The feasting begins with an Easter buffet for the family and invited guests. The table is set with fine heirloom linens and decorated with pussy willow and green, leafy garlands. The symbolic paschal lamb, made of sugar, butter, or, sometimes, babka dough, is placed in the center of the table and often holds a Polish flag to represent victory over death. Cold meats, including roast beef, ham, sausage, veal, turkey, and goose, surround the focal point of the meal—a roast suckling pig. (Leftover meats are made into biros, which is served the following day.) Hard-cooked eggs, sauces, and cwikla, a relish made of beets, sauerkraut, and borscht, accompany the meats. The meal ends with slices of babka and raisin cheesecake, sips of sweet liqueur, and a honey-flavored vodka called krupnik.

Cwikla (Beet Relish)

1 can (16 ounces) whole beets,
   drained and minced
¼ cup prepared horseradish
¼ cup sugar
¼ cup water
¼ cup cider vinegar

1 tablespoon minced
   fresh onion
1 teaspoon salt
⅛ teaspoon coarsely
   ground black pepper

In medium glass bowl, combine all ingredients. Cover and refrigerate several hours or overnight to blend flavors. Serve with cold meats. Makes about 2 cups.

Babka Wielkanocna
(Easter Baba)

1 package active dry yeast
¼ cup warm (not hot) water
4 egg yolks
1 teaspoon salt
½ cup butter
½ cup sugar
½ teaspoon freshly grated
   lemon peel
½ teaspoon cinnamon

4 cups all-purpose flour
1 cup scalded milk, cooled
   to lukewarm
1 cup raisins
fine, dry, unseasoned
   bread crumbs
½ cup finely chopped
   almonds
egg glaze (below)

Dissolve yeast in warm water. Set aside. In small bowl, beat egg yolks and salt until thick and light in color. Set aside. In large bowl, beat butter until softened. Add sugar, and cream well. Blend in beaten egg yolks. Add yeast mixture. Blend in lemon peel and cinnamon. Add flour alternately with milk to egg yolk mixture, beating until smooth. Add raisins. Knead dough in bowl until batter leaves fingers. Cover with damp cloth and let rise in warm place 1½ hours, or until doubled in volume. Generously grease a 10-inch tube or fluted pan. Sprinkle with bread crumbs, turning to coat and lightly tapping to remove any excess crumbs. Punch down dough and place in pan. Cover with damp cloth and let rise again until doubled in volume. Brush with egg glaze. Sprinkle with almonds. Bake at 350 degrees for 30 minutes, or until hollow sounding when tapped. Cool until just warm. Invert onto serving platter and cool completely. Makes 10 to 12 servings.

Egg Glaze: In small bowl, beat 1 egg yolk and 2 tablespoons water with fork. Cover and refrigerate until ready to use.

Ukraine

Foods to Know and Love

Someone advised me against starting any book chapter with a paragraph devoted to my mother-in-law. However, my husband's mother, Kosha (Ukrainian for Catherine), has provided wonderful inspiration for this chapter on Pennsylvania's Ukrainian food heritage. Kosha is 100 percent Ukrainian, and so was her late husband, Walter.

A proud part of the decades of Ukrainian immigrants, Kosh and Walt's parents pressed on to "Ameryka" from Ukraine in the early 1900s to escape the consequences of war and Russia's unbearable political oppression. Most Ukrainian immigrants, ingrained with a strong work ethic, were lured by job opportunities in New York, New Jersey, and Pennsylvania. In fact, Pennsylvania ranks second only to New York in the number of residents claiming Ukrainian descent. Some estimates go as high as 100,000 for the number of Ukrainians living in the commonwealth today. It depends on whom you ask.

Most of the Ukrainian-Americans still live in and around Philadelphia, Pittsburgh, and the northeastern coal-mining regions of the state because that is where their ancestors could find work and prosper. My husband's family chose Philadelphia.

Prior to World War I, Ukraine was known as the "bread basket" of Europe because its rich, black earth and mild climate produced a wealth of grains and vegetables. At that time, about 75 percent of Russian grain exports were grown on Ukrainian soil. After World War I, however, Stalin all but eliminated what he believed to be Ukraine's "rich peasants"—in reality, the Ukrainian agricultural working class—and the once-thriving grain and produce industries began to decline.

As with any food heritage, it's important to mention the history of Ukrainian agriculture because the recipes that are prepared to this day reflect what could be grown in the countryside villages of Ukraine. (By the way, according to family and Ukrainian friends, the correct reference to their country is Ukraine and not "the" Ukraine.)

Wheat flour was a mainstay of the Ukrainian kitchen. The women mixed the freshly milled flour with water or fresh milk, eggs, and salt (a valued commodity in Ukraine), and the resulting dough was rolled and shaped into little pastry pockets called varenyky (pronounced "vah-rin-e-kee") in eastern Ukraine. In western parts of the country, they are called pirohi ("peer-o-hee").

At least once a year, usually around Christmas or Easter, my mother-in-law, Kosh, prepares enough varenyky to feed the entire commonwealth. Kosh carefully measures cupfuls of flour into a well-worn, oversized ceramic bowl. (Why is it that Old World recipes don't seem to work as well when the ingredients are mixed in plastic or aluminum bowls?) Then she adds eggs and cream cheese (for richness) and mixes the dough with a rugged wooden spoon until it "looks right." The dough must be soft, smooth, and manageable under the pressure of a floured rolling pin. The dough is rolled out onto a floured surface to about ¼ inch thickness, then cut into squares or rounds. Generous teaspoonfuls of from-scratch mashed potatoes mixed with cheese or sauerkraut are spooned onto each portion of dough, which is then carefully folded over and sealed shut. The delicate little pasta dumplings are plopped into boiling water and cooked just until tender, drained, and lightly fried in butter or, at the very least, served with melted butter and sour cream as a side dish—certainly not low in fat or calories, but then, what worth eating usually is? Freeze leftovers between layers of waxed paper, tightly sealed in plastic. (It's just as easy to make fifty dozen varenyky at one time as it is to make five, so why not create that floury mess in the kitchen just once a year?)

An important tip: Don't reheat varenyky in the microwave unless you like eating hockey pucks. Thaw these little gems in the refrigerator overnight, then slowly heat through in a skillet that has been lightly coated with a vegetable oil cooking spray.

Kosh's Varenyky (Pirohi)

4 cups all-purpose flour
1 package (3 ounces)
cold cream cheese
4 large eggs
1 teaspoon salt

½ to ¾ cup cold water
about 4 to 5 cups mashed
potatoes
butter
sour cream (optional)

Place flour in large mixing bowl. With pastry blender or fork, cut in cream cheese until coarse crumbs form. In separate bowl, beat together eggs, salt, and ½ cup water. Make a well in the center of the flour-cream cheese mixture. Add egg-water mixture and blend with spoon. Knead on floured board until soft and smooth. (If dough is sticky, add flour to board and knead into dough. If too dry, gradually add up to ¼ cup additional water.) Using floured rolling pin, roll dough about ¼ inch thick on well-floured surface. Cut into approximate 3-inch rounds or squares. Top with rounded teaspoonfuls of mashed potatoes. Fold in half and seal edges. Drop, a few at a time, into rapidly boiling water. Boil, stirring occasionally, 5 minutes or just until tender. Drain and transfer to waxed paper. Fry, a few at a time, in butter until lightly browned. Serve hot with sour cream, if desired. Makes about 4 dozen.

Variations: Add desired amounts of grated cheese or well-drained sauerkraut to mashed potatoes before filling dough.

Ukrainians have always regarded Easter as a time of new beginnings. In the spring, Ukrainian villages would clean, paint, and decorate with delicate, handmade folk motifs in preparation for Velykden ("great day"), or Easter.

As Easter approached, the kitchen became the focal point of the peasant home. Sausages were smoked, cheeses ripened, eggs elaborately decorated, and the contents for *sviachene*, the Easter basket, prepared for a blessing by the parish priest on the steps of the church after the Resurrection service. Small amounts of hard-cooked eggs, butter, cheese, salt, paska or baba (the Easter bread), sausage, and horseradish were required contents of the basket, each symbolizing an important component of the upcoming Easter feast.

Today, Ukrainians continue to carry their symbolic wicker food baskets to Easter mass to be blessed. At home, the sacred contents become part of the hearty feast prepared to celebrate the resurrection of Christ.

While Ukrainian cooks may be best known for making varenyky (and Pennsylvania has several firsthand experts on the subject), lots of other foods closely tied to Ukraine are prepared here in the Keystone State. Borscht (red beet soup), sauerkraut soup, holubtsi (stuffed cabbage), nalysnyky (crepes filled with meat or vegetables), and walnut torte are among the traditional Ukrainian dishes found at various festivals held annually throughout the state. Most such events are organized to promote and maintain the Ukrainian culture and traditions.

In the fall of 1995, I talked with Albina Czapowskyj ("cha-pow-skee") and Olena Karpinich ("car-pin-itch") at the Luzerne County Folk Festival held at the armory in Kingston, Pennsylvania. Kingston is just across the river from Wilkes-Barre and is not an unlikely place for an ethnic festival. After all, Wilkes-Barre, Scranton, Hazleton, and the little villages surrounding them are in the old coal region where many Ukrainians with experience in mining and hard physical labor found appropriate work.

Albina is in her early seventies but looks much younger. She was born in Charkiv, the former capital of Ukraine, and left with her parents after World War II to escape Communism. The family first settled in Morrisville, Pennsylvania, where she learned American customs while holding fast to her European roots. Albina pursued a career as a civil engineering designer, raising two sons with her Ukrainian husband, an environmentalist. Albina was a career woman and working mother long before it was in vogue to be either.

Now a widow, Albina lives in Mountain Top, Pennsylvania, where she continues Ukrainian folk customs—the songs, food, dance, and crafts like those at the armory on the day of my visit. She proudly showed me the Ukrainian exhibit and introduced me to women who were wearing authentic, hand-sewn clothing and speaking fluent Ukrainian. Lavishly decorated Easter eggs, red and black geometric embroidery, well-defined wood carvings, and costumes directly from Ukraine attracted me, especially since prices were reasonable, but my real interest in visiting was the Ukrainian food traditions.

Albina's friend Olena explained that although the Luzerne Folk Festival was probably on its way out, the food would remain available through area churches. She said that Ukrainian Orthodox and Catholic churches in towns and cities across the state are the best source of authentic Ukrainian food, especially varenyky and holubtsi. Just before the Christmas and Easter holidays, she said, many of these churches sell Ukrainian dishes, made to order, at very reasonable prices.

She suggested looking in the yellow pages for church telephone numbers and calling them for more information.

Albina and Olena were armed with their favorite Ukrainian cookbooks. Olena's book, *Ukrainian Cuisine*, was printed in the Soviet Union. Albina's cookbook, apparently the "bible" of Ukrainian cookbooks, was called *Traditional Ukrainian Cookery*, by Savella Stechishin (Trident Press, Ltd., 1959). Albina thought the book may have been reprinted since then, but she preferred her original copy, faded and worn.

The cookbooks contain several versions of traditional Ukrainian dishes. For example, the popular beet soup, or borscht, can be a clear red broth with diced beets or a thick vegetable soup. Seems the heartier version reflects the preferences of eastern Ukraine, while the lighter, brothy version is preferred in the west. Meat was never abundant or widely available in Ukraine, and the country's recipes reflect that. Small amounts of meat may be called for as a garnish, or slivered and stuffed into cabbage (holubtsi) with various combinations of rice, buckwheat, mushrooms, and bread crumbs as filler. Seasonings depend on what is available.

Holubtsi

1 onion, chopped
1 clove garlic, crushed
2 tablespoons butter
1 pound ground beef
¾ cup uncooked white rice
1 teaspoon salt

¼ teaspoon pepper
1 large head cabbage,
   about 3 pounds
1 carrot, sliced
2 cups stewed tomatoes
   or chicken broth

In large skillet, sauté onion and garlic in butter about 5 minutes.
Stir in ground beef, rice, salt, and pepper. Remove from heat
and set aside. Fill large kettle about half full with water. Bring to
boil. Remove and discard core from cabbage. Place cabbage
in kettle of boiling water. Cover and bring to a simmer. Simmer
3 minutes. Remove from heat and cool until easy to handle.
Gently remove outer leaves, using knife to help remove large
center veins from leaves. Arrange a few of the outer cabbage
leaves with the carrot slices on bottom of shallow, oblong baking
dish. Place 2 to 3 tablespoonfuls of beef mixture near stem end
of each additional cabbage leaf. Fold long sides inward, then roll
up, beginning at stem end. Arrange in single layer over cabbage
leaves and carrot slices in dish. Pour stewed tomatoes or chicken
broth over all. Cover with remaining cabbage leaves. Cover
dish with foil. Bake at 350 degrees for 1½ to 2 hours. Makes 6 to
8 servings.

Kievan Borscht

2 quarts beef stock
1 pound fresh beets, peeled
   and diced
1 large onion, chopped
1 turnip, peeled and chopped
2 stalks celery, chopped
1 carrot, chopped
1 clove garlic, crushed
1 bay leaf
½ head cabbage, shredded
1 can whole tomatoes
   (16-ounce size), with liquid

1 can tomato paste
   (6-ounce size)
1 tablespoon snipped
   fresh dill
1 tablespoon snipped
   fresh parsley
1 tablespoon sugar
salt and pepper,
   to taste
sour cream

In large kettle, bring beef stock to boil. Add beets, onion, turnip, celery, carrot, garlic, and bay leaf. Cover and reduce heat. Simmer just until vegetables are tender, stirring occasionally. Add cabbage, tomatoes, tomato paste, dill, parsley, sugar, salt, and pepper. Cover and simmer an additional 15 minutes, or until ready to serve. Top with dollops of sour cream. Makes 8 to 10 servings.

If you don't want to make your own holubtsi, borscht, and varenyky, let someone else do the cooking. My research led to the Society Hill section of Philadelphia, where Ulana Baluch-Mazurkevich owns and operates the somewhat upscale but moderately priced Ulana's Restaurant. Ulana's is tucked below ground in the renovated wine cellar of what used to be a colonial "house of ill repute." (This is, after all, close to the city's old port.)

The menu features contemporary fare and just a few Ukrainian dishes, but they are authentic, adapted from the recipes prepared by Ulana's Ukrainian mother. In an atmosphere of exposed brick and stone, vaulted ceilings, and racks of wine, you can savor a Ukrainian morel mushroom soup prepared with homemade beef stock, vegetables, egg noodles, and a garnish of sour cream. The soup has a naturally woodsy flavor and is not too filling to enjoy as an appetizer. The menu also offers a Ukrainian version of veal with mushrooms, served with a rich sauce of brandy, veal stock, and cream. Varenyky are available, but

Ulana dresses her little potato dumplings with caviar in addition to sour cream.

Ulana also serves a traditional Ukrainian Christmas Eve dinner throughout the first week of January, the week the "old" calendar designates as the Ukrainian Christmas holiday period. Christmas Eve, or *Sviata Vechera*, is celebrated on January 6 and is considered the most important Ukrainian holiday. Food plays an important, very symbolic role in the celebration, and Ulana's has adapted six of the traditional twelve courses that, for decades, have symbolized the apostles.

Although the courses served during the traditional Ukrainian Christmas Eve dinner can vary, depending on specific family traditions, Ulana's menu is a good cross section. It features a traditional borscht soup, ravioli-type pasta stuffed with mushrooms, a herring salad, stuffed cabbage, varenyky, and fish. Dessert is cake with honey or poppy seeds, ingredients often used in Ukrainian sweet breads and pastries.

Ulana's is located at 205 Bainbridge St. in Philadelphia and is open Wednesdays through Saturdays, 5:30 to 11 P.M. The restaurant seats fifty-four, and reservations are recommended. The Ukrainian portion of the menu varies; call (215) 922-4152 for information on specific offerings.

Medianyk (Honey Cake)

½ cup butter
4 large egg yolks
1¼ cups honey
3 cups all-purpose flour
2 teaspoons baking powder
1 teaspoon cinnamon
½ teaspoon ginger

½ teaspoon nutmeg
¼ teaspoon cloves
4 egg whites,
    room temperature
raspberry jam
sweetened whipped cream
grated semisweet chocolate

In large mixer bowl, beat butter to soften. Add egg yolks one at
a time, beating well after each addition. Blend in honey. In
separate bowl, thoroughly combine flour, baking powder, cinnamon, ginger, nutmeg, and cloves. Blend into butter mixture.
In separate clean bowl, beat egg whites until stiff but not dry.
Gradually fold into batter. Pour into lightly greased and floured
9×5-inch loaf pan. Bake at 350 degrees for 1 hour, or until
toothpick inserted in center comes out clean. Cool in pan
15 minutes. Remove and place on wire rack to cool completely.
Slice and serve with raspberry jam, sweetened whipped cream,
and grated chocolate. Makes 8 to 10 servings.

If you feel more like a hoedown than formal dining in the city, slip on
your casual clothes and drive upstate to Osela Oleha Olzhycha, the
Ukrainian Homestead, in Lehighton, Pennsylvania, off Route 209 South,
about 3 miles southwest of Jim Thorpe. This family-oriented resort, or
osela, was named in memory of Oleh Olzhych, a World War II Ukrainian
political activist, patriot, and poet, and encompasses a campsite, two
dance halls, a Byzantine chapel (with masses every Sunday), a summer
restaurant, a bar, bungalow-type apartments, a motel, and a swimming pool.

The homestead was purchased in 1956 by the Organization for the
Rebirth of Ukraine for the purpose of maintaining the Ukrainian heritage in this country. Although the homestead's 200 members are primarily Ukrainian families and descendants, anyone can attend the
various events held throughout the warmer months.

Memorial Day weekend offers the first in a series of summer activities at the homestead that include traditional Ukrainian folk dances,
music, food, and dress, but most homesteaders consider July 4 the offi-
cial kickoff to weekend festivities that run through Labor Day. The

largest event, a Ukrainian folk festival, is held every year on the third weekend in August to commemorate the freedom of Ukraine. Starting at noon on festival weekend, vendors set up shop to sell Ukrainian folk art at modest prices. The menu, prepared by the homestead's chef, includes borscht, stuffed cabbage, sausage (kovbasa) with sauerkraut, and, as always, varenyky. You can top off these selections with a generous slice of the traditional Ukrainian torte, three layers of rich walnut cake filled with vanilla custard and finished with a bittersweet chocolate icing. Pampushky, the Ukrainian doughnut, is available, too. Then go to one of the evening dances as a way to work off those calories. The festival admission is $5.

In October, the homestead hosts touring dance ensembles from Ukraine. Traditional Ukrainian fare is sold during the performances. Admission is $12. Call for a schedule of performances.

The Ukrainian Homestead is located at 230 Beaver Run Rd., Lehighton, PA 18235. Call (610) 377-4621 on weekends or (215) 235-3709 during the week for information.

Manor Junior College in Jenkintown is just a few city miles north of center-city Philadelphia. This two-year liberal-arts college was founded by the Sisters of Saint Basil, a Ukrainian-Catholic order of nuns. To preserve Ukrainian history and culture and educate the community, especially children, about the Ukrainian heritage, the school organized a Ukrainian festival eighteen years ago. The festival is held every year on the first Sunday afternoon in October and features demonstrations, exhibits, literature, and a variety of children's activities.

The festival draws 3,000 to 4,000 people from as far away as Florida with the authenticity of its folk art, music, dancing, and food. Recent Manor College festivals have boasted demonstrations by master craftsmen in the art of bead weaving, an intricate and specialized Ukrainian skill that requires years of practice. You'll see colorfully beaded necklaces and belts worn by vendors and dancers, as well as the craftsmen.

There is plenty of excellent food—sausage with sauerkraut, varenyky, and rich baked goods donated by local Ukrainians. I had cabbage stuffed with meat and rice and topped with a delicious mushroom sauce. The borscht was generally served with vushka, or "little ears" of mushroom-stuffed dough, as a special ingredient. This is the traditional way to prepare borscht for the Ukrainian Christmas Eve supper. All of the food is reasonably priced. The festival admission is $4 per adult and $1 per child.

Manor College also holds a minifestival three Sundays before Easter to display pysanky, traditional Ukrainian Easter eggs. There is a small admission fee, but it's well worth the cost to see this beautiful art form (also for sale) and enjoy traditional Ukrainian food.

Manor Junior College is at 700 Fox Chase Rd., Jenkintown, PA 19046. For information on upcoming events, call (215) 885-2360.

The Cathedral of Learning, a forty-two-story, Gothic stone sky-scraper, seems to anchor the University of Pittsburgh campus. At the Ukrainian Renaissance Festival held there, on the grassy knoll where Forbes, Bellefield, and Fifth Avenues converge with Bigelow Boulevard, you can enjoy Ukrainian food, music, and customs.

More than 4,000 people attend the Ukrainian festival in Pitts-burgh, whose Ukrainian population is estimated as high as 40,000. It takes a virtual food factory of volunteers in the kitchens of supporting Catholic and Orthodox churches to produce all the necessary amounts of authentic Ukrainian dishes that become an integral part of the fes-tival. A single parish may contribute 150 dozen varenyky—that's 1,800 dumplings.

The Pittsburgh version of varenyky is usually stuffed with a blend of mashed potatoes and sautéed onions. A noodle and cabbage casse-role (lokshyna z kapustoiu), prepared by St. Mary's down the street, is delicious and unusual. So is the apple-noodle casserole (lokshyna z iablukamy), flavored with cinnamon and a touch of sugar. A buttery, seasoned chicken breast sandwich, borscht, and a vinaigrette salad make an inexpensive but very satisfying meal. Stuffed cabbage, sausage, and sauerkraut are also available. Food prices begin at 50 cents (per varenyky), and for $5, you'll get a broad sampling of most items.

About a dozen vendors display and sell Ukrainian clothing, jewelry, needlework, leather items, and hand-crafted folk art, including ceramic pottery and lavishly decorated eggs. Limited-edition and one-of-a-kind works by master craftsmen are expensive, but many items are very rea-sonable and within reach of the average visitor.

This free, family-oriented festival is held Saturday and Sunday afternoons on the last weekend of September. Allow yourself time to visit the Ukrainian Room in the Cathedral of Learning. It's one of twenty-three "nationality rooms" that represent a grass-roots commu-nity effort to promote cultural diversity in and around Pittsburgh through exhibits and architecture.

For more information on the Ukrainian Renaissance Festival and the Nationality Rooms, write The Nationality Room Program, Cathe-dral of Learning, University of Pittsburgh, Pittsburgh, PA 15213 or call (412) 624-6000.

Noodles with Apples

6 large, tart apples
2 tablespoons sugar
1 teaspoon cinnamon
dash salt
8 ounces egg noodles,
    uncooked

3 tablespoons fine, dry,
    unseasoned bread
    crumbs (divided)
1 tablespoon vegetable oil
vegetable oil
    cooking spray

Peel, core, and grate apples into large bowl. Add sugar, cinnamon, and salt, tossing until apples are coated; set aside. Cook noodles according to package directions. (Do not overcook.) Rinse and drain well. In skillet, sauté 2 tablespoons of the bread crumbs in oil until lightly browned. Add to noodles. Lightly coat a large casserole dish with cooking spray. Sprinkle with remaining tablespoon bread crumbs. Alternate layers of noodle-crumb mixture with apple-cinnamon mixture in casserole, ending with noodle mixture. Bake at 350 degrees for 45 minutes. Serve hot as an entrée or side dish. Makes 6 to 8 servings.

Fresh Egg Noodles and Cabbage

1 cup all-purpose flour
3 large eggs, slightly beaten
1 tablespoon water
1 teaspoon salt
3 tablespoons fine, dry,
    unseasoned bread crumbs

2 cups shredded cabbage
1 medium onion, chopped
¼ cup butter, divided
½ teaspoon salt
¼ teaspoon freshly
    ground pepper

In large bowl, mix flour, eggs, water, and salt until rough ball forms. Knead on floured surface 10 to 15 minutes, or until smooth. (If dough is too stiff, add 1 to 2 tablespoons additional water, as needed.) Let rest 5 minutes. Knead an additional 5 minutes. Let rest 5 minutes more. Using floured rolling pin, roll out dough about ¼ inch thick on well-floured surface. Flip and let stand 15 to 20 minutes. Flip again and let stand another 15 minutes, flouring surface well before turning. Cut into strips ½ inch wide. Arrange on lightly floured, clean towel to dry for about 15 minutes. Then drop noodles in boiling water, stirring occasionally and cooking until done, about 4 minutes. (Do not overcook.) Rinse and drain. In large skillet, sauté bread crumbs in 1 tablespoon of the butter until lightly browned. Remove from skillet and set aside. Sauté cabbage and onion in remaining butter until tender. Add salt and pepper. Toss with cooked noodles and heat through. Sprinkle with bread crumbs. Serve hot as a side dish. Makes 6 to 8 servings.

Pickled Watermelon Rind

3 pounds watermelon rind
salted water
4 cups sugar
3 cups white vinegar
six 3-inch cinnamon sticks

2 tablespoons whole cloves
2 tablespoons whole allspice
2 tablespoons whole
   mustard seeds

Cut watermelon rind into 1-inch cubes. Peel off and discard outer skin and any pink flesh. Place rind in large bowl. Cover with salted water. Cover and refrigerate overnight. Drain and set aside. In large kettle or Dutch oven, combine sugar and vinegar. Bring to boil. Bundle cinnamon sticks, cloves, allspice, and mustard seeds in 4 layers of clean cheesecloth. Tie closed with string. Place in the sugar-vinegar mixture with the drained watermelon rind. Cook, uncovered, 45 minutes, or until rind is transparent. Remove and discard spice bundle. Pack watermelon rind in sterile glass jars. Completely cover with hot cooking liquid and to within ⅛ inch of jar top. Seal tightly with sterile lids. Cool. Refrigerate until ready to use. Makes about 6 cups.

Stuffed Tomatoes

4 medium tomatoes
2 tablespoons butter
⅓ cup chopped onion
½ pound ground beef
1 cup cooked white rice
⅓ cup sour cream
1 tablespoon snipped fresh dill

½ teaspoon salt
¼ teaspoon coarsely
  ground black pepper
fine, dry, unseasoned
  bread crumbs

Core and seed tomatoes, leaving whole. In large skillet, melt butter over medium high heat. Add onions. Sauté 3 minutes. Add ground beef. Cook and stir until browned. Drain off any excess cooking liquid. Stir in rice, sour cream, dill, salt, and pepper. Spoon rice mixture into tomato "shells." Sprinkle with bread crumbs. Arrange in shallow baking dish. Cover and bake at 375 degrees for 20 minutes. Remove cover and bake additional 10 minutes, or until tomatoes are tender. Serve immediately. Makes 4 servings.

Dark Rye Bread

2 cups scalded milk
2 tablespoons butter
2 tablespoons sugar
1 teaspoon salt
1 pakcage active dry yeast

½ cup warm (not hot) water
4 cups rye flour, divided
2½ cups whole-wheat flour
2 tablespoons caraway seeds

In large bowl, pour scalded milk over butter, sugar, and salt. Stir. Set aside to cool. Dissolve yeast in warm water. Add yeast mixture and 3 cups of the rye flour to milk mixture, mixing well. Beat in remaining 1 cup rye flour with wooden spoon. Cover with damp cloth and let rise in warm place 1 to 1½ hours, or until doubled in volume. Turn out onto floured surface. Knead in whole-wheat flour and caraway seeds. Knead until dough is smooth. Divide dough into two equal portions. Shape each portion into a round loaf. Place on lightly greased baking sheet. Cover with damp cloth and let rise in warm place until doubled in volume. Bake at 450 degrees for 15 minutes. Reduce oven to 350 degrees, and bake additional 35 to 40 minutes, or until bread sounds hollow when lightly tapped. Cool. Makes 2 large loaves.

Ireland and Scotland

A Passion for Food and Lore

The Irish and Scottish influence on Pennsylvania's rich food heritage began with the large-scale immigration of these groups to the American colonies during the early 1600s. Celtic groups (those from Ireland, Scotland, Brittany, Cornwall, the Isle of Mann, and Wales) settled in all of the colonies. They preferred Pennsylvania, however, because unlike the surrounding colonies, she imposed fewer laws restricting religious freedom. Pennsylvania's Irish and Scottish settlements grew throughout the next two centuries and were bolstered in the mid-1800s by immigrants fleeing the potato famine, which was ravaging their beloved homelands at the time.

During the early 1900s, many Irish and Scottish immigrants were drawn to cities like Philadelphia and Pittsburgh, where they could set up shops and pubs. Others found jobs in the state's farmlands and anthracite coal regions. All were preoccupied with finding steady work and building churches.

The Irish and Scottish immigrants mainstreamed well in Pennsylvania, but at the same time, they clung to their centuries-old traditions, including methods of food preparation. Recipes on crumpled brown paper, shipped from home in hand-carved wooden boxes, helped bridge old customs with the less comfortable and unfamiliar ways of life in the States. "Comfort foods," as we describe them today, helped the immigrants cope with the unknown.

Southern fried chicken, one of America's most popular comfort foods, is Scottish in origin, brought to Virginia and the Carolinas by Scottish immigrants in the mid to late 1700s. Potatoes ("tatties") were the staple of the traditional Celtic diet—no surprise there. And oatmeal ("stirabout"), seasoned with a dash of salt and cooked into a thick, hot porridge, was a substantial breakfast on Irish and Scottish tables. Rich meat stews, vegetable soups, and seafood, including smoked salmon, were favorites. Recipes for these varied from family to family and across generations, depending on each cook's ingredient preferences and kitchen technique.

The Scottish have their haggis, a pudding made from the heart, liver, and other organs of the sheep. The ingredients are chopped and mixed with onions and oatmeal, then stuffed into a sheep's stomach and boiled. Served with potatoes and a dram of whiskey, it's a unique meal, to say the very least, but a national symbol of Scotland. Many Scots will tell you that haggis is similar to Philadelphia scrapple.

The Irish have their own unusual recipes, including drisheens, made from sheep's blood, chopped mutton suet, milk, and bread crumbs, and Dublin is the origin of coddle, a mixture of cooked bacon, sausages, onions, and potatoes. On Halloween, the most traditional of Irish-Americans will prepare colcannon, a blend of kale or cabbage and mashed potatoes. A coin is tucked inside to symbolize good luck for the one who finds it. Irish stew is familiar to most of us. This simple but hearty blend of lamb, potatoes, onions, and meat stock has mass appeal, but Irishman Dick Coakley, proprietor of Coakley's Restaurant and Pub in New Cumberland, says conservative Pennsylvanians prefer beef to lamb in their Irish stew.

Maggie's Irish Stew

2½ pounds potatoes,
   peeled and sliced
1½ pounds uncooked lamb or
   beef, cubed
1 medium onion, chopped
salt and pepper, to taste

2 tablespoons snipped
   fresh parsley
1 bay leaf
2 cups boiling water or
   meat stock

In large heavy pot, place a third of the potatoes and top with a third of the lamb or beef and a third of the onion. Season with salt and pepper. Repeat layers two more times. Add parsley and bay leaf. Pour boiling water or stock over top. Cover and bring to boil. Reduce heat. Simmer, covered and stirring occasionally, about 2½ hours, or until lamb is tender and most of the liquid is absorbed. Makes 6 servings.

Colcannon

1 cup milk
½ cup butter, divided
1 carrot, chopped
1 bay leaf
1 large onion, chopped
1 bunch fresh kale, rinsed
    and chopped

4 pounds potatoes,
    peeled and cubed
cold water
salt and pepper, to taste

In medium saucepan, combine milk, 2 tablespoons of the butter, carrot, and bay leaf. Cover and bring to a simmer. Remove from heat and set aside. In large Dutch oven, melt 1 tablespoon of the butter. Add onion. Sauté over medium heat about 8 minutes, or until lightly browned. Add kale. Cover and cook, stirring occasionally, over medium heat about 25 minutes or until tender. Meanwhile, in separate pot, cover potatoes with cold water. Cover and bring to boil. Cook 25 to 30 minutes or until tender. Remove from heat and drain well. Return to pot and mash. Add cooked kale. Strain milk mixture to remove carrot and bay leaf. Stir milk into potato-kale mixture. Season with salt and pepper. Transfer to hot serving bowl. Keep warm. Melt remaining 5 tablespoons butter. Spoon over potato mixture in bowl. Serve immediately. Makes 8 servings.

Baked goods are the best known and most traditional of Irish and Scottish foods. Boxty bread, an Irish potato bread, is marked with a cross and eaten on Halloween or All Saint's Day as a form of religious protection from evil. The Irish bury a ring in barmbrack, an unleavened cake made with raisins and currants, and offer slices to those who are single. The person who receives the slice containing the ring is expected to be married within a year.

Irish soda bread is prepared with flour, baking soda, and buttermilk. Sometimes raisins are added to the batter before baking. In the old country, the bread is baked in a *bastable,* an oven heated by a bed of glowing hot coals. As a result, soda bread is also known as bastable cake in some parts of Ireland.

I had fun making Irish soda bread in my own kitchen using my modern electric oven. It was extremely easy, perfect for novice bakers and "Type A" folks with little time to spare. Of course, I couldn't leave the original recipe alone. I substituted buttermilk powder and water for the fresh buttermilk specified in the old version. (The remnants of Hurricane Fran—reduced to a heavy rain—were swirling up outside, so a trip to the store just to buy buttermilk seemed frivolous.) I had the dough mixed and ready for the oven in 10 minutes. The result was a deliciously dense Old World hearth bread.

Irish Soda Bread

3 cups stone-ground whole-wheat flour
⅓ cup buttermilk powder
1½ teaspoons salt

1 teaspoon baking soda
1¼ cups water
1 cup raisins, optional

In large bowl, thoroughly combine whole-wheat flour, buttermilk powder, salt, and baking soda. Stir in water. Add raisins, if desired. Transfer to 2 lightly greased 8- or 9-inch round cake pans. Shape into tall round loaves. Cover loosely with lightly greased aluminum foil. Bake at 450 degrees for 30 minutes. Remove foil. Bake an additional 10 minutes, or until lightly browned. Remove from pan. Serve warm, or cool on wire rack. Makes 2 loaves.

The Scottish have their own baked goods, often similar to those favored by the Irish. Flavorful oatcake biscuits can be either savory, like the Bara Ceirch recipe below, or sweet, like those served at the Telegraph House restaurant in San Francisco. Fragrant yeast buns called baps, also known as morning rolls or fadge, are considered the national roll of Scotland, and buttery, rich shortbread cookies are usually served with tea. Slices of bannock, a lard-based fruit cake, are common on the Scottish dessert tray and reminiscent of stollen.

Scottish Bannock

4 to 5 cups unbleached
    flour, divided ·
1½ cups warm (not hot) water
2 teaspoons salt
1 package active dry yeast
1 cup sweet (unsalted)
    butter, softened
½ cup lard, softened

1 cup sugar
1 pound raisins
½ pound currants
½ pound chopped dried
    apricots
½ teaspoon fresh
    orange zest

In large bowl, combine 1 cup of the flour, warm water, salt, and yeast. Set aside. In separate bowl, cream butter, lard, and sugar until light and fluffy. Add to flour-yeast mixture, blending well. Gradually add remaining flour, ½ cup at a time, until smooth dough forms. Stir in raisins, currants, apricots, and orange zest. Transfer dough to floured surface. Knead about 8 minutes, or until very smooth and elastic. Divide into 3 equal portions. Shape into smooth rounds. Place in three lightly greased 8-inch round cake pans. Cover with damp cloth. Let rise at room temperature 30 minutes. Meanwhile, position rack in center of oven. Preheat to 350 degrees. Bake 1 to 1½ hours, or just until loaves sound hollow when lightly thumped. (If bread begins to brown too quickly, cover with foil.) Remove from pans. Cool on wire racks. Wrap tightly until ready to slice. Makes 3 loaves.

Oatcakes (Bara Ceirch)

2 cups uncooked old-fashioned
  oats, divided
2 tablespoons sweet
  (unsalted) butter

½ teaspoon salt
⅓ cup hot water

In food processor, combine 1½ cups of the oats, butter, and salt. Process 15 seconds, or just until mixture resembles coarse crumbs. Gradually add hot water, processing 10 seconds, or just until blended. Transfer dough to surface that has been sprinkled with about 3 tablespoons of the remaining oats. Flatten dough to 5-inch-diameter circle. Sprinkle with additional 3 tablespoons of the remaining oats. Roll dough to ⅛ inch thickness with lightly floured rolling pin. Using 2½-inch round biscuit or cookie cutter, cut dough into rounds. Transfer to baking sheet that has been lightly sprinkled with remaining oats. Bake at 350 degrees for 20 to 25 minutes, or just until edges begin to brown. Serve warm or reheat in microwave just before serving. Makes about 2 dozen.

Orange Shortbread Cookies

2 cups sweet (unsalted)
  butter, softened
1½ cups firmly packed light
  brown sugar
freshly grated zest of
  2 small oranges

4 cups unbleached flour
⅛ teaspoon salt
2 eggs
2 tablespoons water

In large bowl, cream butter, brown sugar, and orange zest. In separate bowl, combine flour and salt. Gradually blend into creamed mixture. Cover and refrigerate at least 2 hours. Line baking sheets with parchment paper. Transfer dough to lightly floured surface. Roll dough to ½ inch thickness with lightly floured rolling pin. Using 2-inch cookie cutters, cut dough into desired shapes. Place on parchment-lined baking sheets. In small bowl, beat eggs and water. Brush onto cookies. Bake at 350 degrees for 16 to 18 minutes, or until very lightly browned. Cool slightly on baking sheets. Transfer to wire racks and cool completely. Makes about 5 dozen.

If you enjoy baking and want to pursue some new recipes, try *From Celtic Hearts*, a neat little cookbook by Deborah Krasner. You'll find easy-to-follow recipes for baked goods from Scotland, Ireland, and Wales. The book is published by Viking Penguin, a division of Penguin Books USA Inc., and retails for $9.95.

The Valley Forge Convention Center houses greater Philadelphia's Scottish and Irish Festival one midwinter weekend a year and attracts hundreds of folk, primarily from New Jersey, New York, and Pennsylvania. The festival's focus is on Scottish and Irish music and dancing—folk singers, pipe bands, and troubadours—and you can learn a great deal about Celtic heritage from the exhibits and literature that line the main convention hall. There are dozens of books, authentic handmade crafts, special-interest groups, and vendors eager to tout the history of Ireland and Scotland.

When I attended the festival, the volume of information available to the public was abundant, almost overwhelming. The extent of Scottish and Irish food, on the other hand, was a little disappointing, but the quality and authenticity were excellent. Argyle Restaurant of

Kearny, New Jersey, offered traditional fish and chips, properly crisp-fried but not greasy. The festival offered a modest assortment of other classic Celtic foods, including meat pies and soda bread at very reasonable prices. Diane and Frank Donovan, proprietors of F. J. Donovan's catering, featured Irish pastries. I took home a generous bag of their delicious raisin scones, similar to baking powder biscuits and a cornerstone of Ireland's abundant baked goods. The scones were delicious reheated in the microwave, then slathered with generous spoonfuls of strawberry jam.

Admission to the Valley Forge Scottish and Irish Festival is $12 at the door for adults and $10 for advance tickets. Children under 12 are admitted free. There is no charge for parking. The Valley Forge Convention Center is located just off Exit 24 of the Pennsylvania Turnpike. Follow the Convention Center signs to Route 363 (Gulph Road) and First Avenue.

Fried Potato Skins

1 cup all-purpose flour	water
¼ teaspoon salt	scrubbed skins from
⅛ teaspoon coarsely ground	3 large potatoes
black pepper	vegetable oil

In large, shallow bowl, combine flour, salt, and pepper. Add water a tablespoon at a time, blending with fork until stiff batter forms. Dip potato skins in flour mixture, coating completely. Fill a large saucepan or deep-fat fryer one-third full with oil. Heat to 190 degrees. Slide potato skins, a few at a time, into hot oil. Fry until crisp. Drain on paper-towel-lined plate. Serve hot. Makes 4 to 6 servings.

Edinboro University is about 15 miles south of Erie and is best known for its educational and arts programs. Founded in 1856 by Scottish settlers, this school of about 8,000 students hosts a Spring Highlands Festival during the first weekend in May.

Edinboro's event is quite impressive, with plenty of Scottish games and exhibitions like sheepherding, and there's golf, volleyball, mountain biking, softball, and tug-of-war, too. If you're not up to athletics, just relax and enjoy the parade of tartans, piping and drumming, dance competition, Scottish clan exhibits, and vendors.

I talked food with Edinboro's festival director, Tim Thompson. He said there's plenty to eat at the festival and the campus chefs have thoughtfully researched Celtic culinary traditions in preparation for the event. For just a couple dollars, you can sample lamb and sausage pies, shepherd's pie, roast chicken with potatoes, and pastries like empire biscuits, tarts, and eccle cakes. Thompson stressed that those festival foods are certainly good but said that the Ceilidh (pronounced "kay-lee"), a Scottish party, boasts the best food and drink of the weekend.

For about $20, you'll enter the Ceilidh and get a full Celtic meal including haggis, with all the ceremony that surrounds this beloved pudding made from sheep organs. Dinner opens with a seventeenth-century poem called "To a Haggis," devoted to this revered dish. A fully costumed Old World Scottish gentleman reads the lyrics after the haggis is marched in and paraded around the room on an oversized platter. With bagpipes wailing, the Scotsman addresses the haggis, then stabs it in preparation for serving. A shot of whiskey follows, and the guests enjoy the feast. By the way, Edinboro's haggis is made by Opies Restaurant in Hamilton, Ontario. Owner and former Scottish soccer champ Danny McLardy makes 50 pounds of haggis just for the Edinboro Ceilidh.

The Edinboro Spring Highlands Games are held the first weekend in May at the school's athletic facility and grounds. Events are scheduled Friday from 1 to 9 P.M. and Saturday from 9 A.M. to 6:30 P.M. General admission is $5 per adult and $2 for children and seniors. The Ceilidh is held at the close of Saturday's activities and requires separate tickets for admission. For further information, contact Edinboro University at (800) 526-0121.

Bread Pudding with Whiskey Sauce

12 slices white bread,
 lightly toasted
¼ cup butter, softened
½ cup raisins
2 eggs
3 tablespoons sugar

1¼ cups milk
1¼ cups heavy or
 whipping cream
1 tablespoon vanilla extract
whiskey sauce (below)

Using 2-inch biscuit cutter, cut 2 rounds from each slice of toast. Spread with softened butter. Place a round in bottom of 4 lightly greased ramekins. Sprinkle with a third of the raisins. Top with another slice of the toast rounds. Sprinkle with another third of raisins and top with remaining toast rounds. In large bowl, whisk together eggs and sugar. Whisk in milk, cream, and vanilla. Spoon mixture over toast-raisin layers in ramekins. Arrange in large roasting pan. Pour water around ramekins to depth of about 1 inch. Bake at 350 degrees for 45 minutes to 1 hour, or until almost set. Cool and serve slightly warm with hot whiskey sauce. Makes 4 servings.

Whiskey Sauce: In small saucepan, melt ½ cup plus 1 tablespoon sweet (unsalted) butter over medium heat. Add sugar. Cook and stir until dissolved. Reduce heat to low. Whisk in 1 beaten egg, blending well. Cook 1 minute, stirring constantly. Remove from heat. Blend in 2 tablespoons Irish whiskey. Serve hot.

Droves of Scots living in and around the Delaware Valley participate in the thirty-year-old Delco Scottish Games. The caber toss (formerly referred to as "ye tossing of ye bar") is the most popular attraction at the games. To cheers from the grandstand, brawny athletes called "heavies" toss the caber, a 100- to 130-pound pole that looks very much like a giant tree trunk. The object is to see who can flip the caber end-over-end with the most precision.

Bagpipes are always an important part of the games, since Scottish clans identify closely with this form of music. There are plenty of pipe and drum bands parading the grounds to entertain the masses. People enjoy highland dancing, singing, historical displays about Scotland, sheepdog demonstrations, Scottish crafts, and of course, the food.

At a food hut called The Flavour of Britain, the proprietor was an older, distinguished Englishman. He explained that the lines between English and Scottish foods have blurred through the generations and offered lots of fancy little pastries, cakes, and buns that could represent either country. (Food historians also emphasize the French influence on Scotland's recipes, as evidenced in the country's love of rich pastries.)

I liked The Flavour of Britain's dundee cake, a rich fruit cake, and empress biscuits, which were shortbread cookies filled with raspberry jam. One main-dish item called a Cornish pasty was a golden, flaky crust filled with beef, potatoes, carrots, and onions, most likely a spinoff of the classic Irish and Scottish meat pies. The Flavour of Britain has a retail shop, tearoom, and catering business in Wilmington, Delaware, but travels to various Irish and Scottish events in Pennsylvania. You can find it on the Internet at http://www.britannia.com.

Argyle's Fish and Chips and F. J. Donovan's also were at the Delco games, as was Cameron's of Kearny, which advertised meat pies, bridies (another flaky pastry), and sausage rolls as their house specialties.

Tickets for the Delco games cost about $10 for adults and $3 for children. Parking prices vary. This is a Saturday event held in mid-June at the Linvilla Orchards in Media from 9:00 A.M. to 6:00 P.M.

The Valley Forge festival and Delco games are two of several Celtic events sponsored by East of the Hebrides Entertainments, a Pennsylvania-based company that specializes in entertainment to enlighten the public about Irish and Scottish customs and culture. This company organizes a variety of other events throughout Pennsylvania each year. You can call East of the Hebrides Entertainment at (610) 825-7268 for dates and further information.

Scottish clans from all parts of the United States have gathered at the Ligonier Highland Games for almost forty years now. Neighboring Fort Ligonier, not by coincidence, is one of many sites where Scottish general John Forbes and his 5,000 British and Scottish troops garrisoned themselves during the French and Indian War.

Held the first Saturday after Labor Day at Idlewild Park, the Ligonier games include activities ranging from the caber toss to highland dancing. These Scottish games are similar to other highland games held throughout the country, but there is one significant difference: Ligonier features Smith's Bakery, a family owned and operated Scottish business in nearby Wilkinsburg.

In 1961, Roy Smith made just $13 his first day as a bakery owner and immediately questioned the wisdom of his new venture. He became a successful baker by filling a regional niche: the demand for authentic Celtic pastries among the descendants of Scottish immigrants who had first settled in and around Pittsburgh during the mid-1700s. Smith's bakery and the Ligonier games remain a perfect marriage after more than thirty-five years. Games organizer David Peet says, "Smith's makes the best meat pies I've ever tasted"—quite an endorsement from a Scottish descendant who claims to have eaten many a meat pie in his day.

Roy Smith won't get too specific about his treasured family formulas for items like meat pie and eccle cake, a rich, fat-laden pastry usually served at breakfast. Roy's empire biscuit, a rich breakfast shortbread, and fern cake, made from pie dough, almonds, and an apple-raspberry filling, are also made with some top-secret ingredients. You'll have to go to the Ligonier games to taste them, but don't expect Roy to share the recipes.

For more information on the Ligonier Highland Games, call Idlewild Park (on U.S. Route 30) at (412) 238-3666.

Bacon, Egg, and Onion Pie

unbaked crust for 9-inch pie	⅔ cup heavy or
2 tablespoons butter	whipping cream
1 large onion, chopped	⅓ cup milk
¼ cup snipped fresh parsley	¼ teaspoon salt
6 slices uncooked bacon, cut up	¼ teaspoon pepper
3 large eggs	⅛ teaspoon nutmeg

Transfer pie crust to 9-inch pie plate or tart pan with removable bottom. Crimp edge in decorative pattern. Prick bottom and side of crust with fork. Bake at 425 degrees for 10 minutes. Set aside. Reduce oven to 400 degrees. In large skillet, melt butter. Add onion and parsley and sauté for 3 minutes. Spoon into crust. In same skillet, cook bacon until crisp, stirring occasionally. Drain on paper towels. Spoon over onion mixture in crust. In small bowl, beat eggs, cream, milk, salt, pepper, and nutmeg just until blended. Pour over mixture in crust. Bake at 400 degrees for 25 minutes, or until set. Cool slightly. Serve warm. Makes 6 servings.

Downtown Pittsburgh's Station Square is home for an Irish festival the second weekend in September. (That particular weekend falls midway between St. Patrick's Day of each year.) Hosted by the Pittsburgh Brewing Company, this festival has its own amphitheater and beer tent, and also features Irish tea for those who don't want to imbibe. You can enjoy an Irish marketplace and learn about the country's geography, history, music, and lore within the various tents erected for the weekend. The festival also offers a Sunday morning mass in Gaelic, the earliest language of the Irish, at the amphitheater.

Food vendors from greater Pittsburgh include Mr. O'Salvatore, an Italian gentleman who adds an O to his last name just for the weekend. Vendors offer Irish classics like ham and cabbage, Guinness-braised beef, and potato soup, as well as shepherd's pie (a casserole of mashed potatoes and lamb, veal, or beef), Dublin coddle (a savory bacon called tinne or senshaille in Ireland), and sausage stew. Traditional baked goods—boxty pancakes, soda bread, and the rest—as well as Joyce's Copper Kettle Fudge, are there to eat on the spot or take home. If you're not in the mood for Irish, you can get meatballs or pizza instead. Food prices compete nicely with those at other Celtic events throughout the state.

Weekend passes at $12 per person are available for Pittsburgh's Irish festival. Daily tickets cost $5 per adult and $2 for children. For more information, write the Pittsburgh Irish Festival, Inc., P.O. Box 81173, Pittsburgh, PA 15217, or call (412) 422-5642.

Dublin Coddle

4 cups (1 quart) water
1 pound uncooked pork
    sausage links, cut up
8 thick slices uncooked
    bacon, cut up
2 pounds potatoes, peeled
    and sliced

4 large onions, chopped
¼ cup snipped fresh
    parsley
salt and pepper, to taste

In large pot, bring water to a boil. Add sausage and bacon.
Reduce heat. Cover and simmer 6 to 8 minutes. Drain and
reserve cooking liquid. Toss sausage and bacon with potatoes,
onions, parsley, salt, and pepper. Transfer to large casserole dish.
Spoon just enough of the reserved cooking liquid over top to
almost cover. Bake at 200 degrees for 1 hour, or until potatoes
are tender and liquid is reduced by about half. Serve hot. Makes
6 to 8 servings.

Bethlehem's September Celtic Classic Highland Games, sponsored by
Celtic Fest, Inc., draw a huge crowd of almost 150,000 people. Yes, you'll
be shoulder-to-shoulder, but you'll truly enjoy the Celtic games, music,
dancing, and bagpipes. The kids will certainly love the crafts, too.

The Bethlehem event offers an impressive spread of authentic
Scottish and Irish food by area vendors. In the Grand Pavilion, look for
Bray's Ethnic Foods, whose corned beef and cabbage stew and saffron
cake are delicious. Deschler's Seafood has an excellent crab pattie, as
well as breaded haddock and scallop platters, clam strips, and oyster
sandwiches. Be sure to sample Dublin Provision Company's corned
beef, Irish stew, or shepherd's pie, or have an Irish coffee with breakfast
at the Donegal Square concession.

Bethlehem's Tavern in the Glen has its own food concessions as a
part of the Celtic fest. Stewart's of Kearney has meat pies, sausage rolls,
bridies, assorted scones and Scottish cakes, and soda bread. E-Clare's
bakes up rich and tempting specialty desserts with just a touch of the
Irish: chocolate mint brownies, chocolate mint kisses, tortes, and cakes.

On the parade grounds, you'll find the International Gourmet, with
classic haggis, bridies, meat pies, and such, and if you're not in the
mood for Irish, there's plenty of the usual carnival-type fare, including

funnel cake, hot dogs, steak sandwiches, and tacos. Food prices are on par with those at other events of this kind.

The Celtic Classic Highland Games are held near the historic, pre-Revolutionary War settlement area of Bethlehem during the last weekend of each September, Friday from 5 to 11 P.M., Saturday from 9 A.M. to 11 P.M., and Sunday from 10 A.M. to 8 P.M. There is no admission to the event, but you will need to pay for municipal parking. For more information, call Celtic Fest, Inc., at (610) 868-9599.

The Pocono Manor Inn is a charming, old-fashioned resort hotel secluded in the mountains of northeastern Pennsylvania. During a three-day weekend in March and November, the inn rolls out its semi-annual Irish Extravaganza.

More than 400 people, most from Pennsylvania, New York, New Jersey, and Maryland, attend the Irish Extravaganza to celebrate their heritage and love affair with Irish tradition. Hotel guests check in Friday evening in time for dinner and check out just after brunch on Sunday. Few feel compelled to leave the self-contained resort during their Irish weekend stay, since the package price of about $230 per person includes meals and entertainment.

Guests enjoy a full weekend of Irish entertainment, including music, singing, dancing, and a fashion show sponsored by Ireland's Brannigan Weavers. John Cronin, who coordinates the event for the hotel, owns Cronin's Irish Cottage, a gourmet shop in Scranton, which boasts a large Irish population. Cronin and other area vendors set up temporary shop in the Pocono Manor Inn's lobby to sell their wares, including imported Irish food, wool blends, Waterford crystal and Belleek china, Irish cookbooks, jewelry, sweatshirts, and trinkets. Prices range from a few dollars up to about $400.

The hotel staff describes the menu as "American cuisine with an Irish touch." Chefs Alan Green and Bob Compton serve up roast leg of lamb, steak and kidney pie, and liver with bacon and onions for meals most of us would consider well beyond a "touch" of Irish fare. Ingredients for this authentic cuisine are Irish imports, a good excuse to fall off a low-fat diet for at least one weekend each year.

For more information, contact the Pocono Manor Inn and Golf Resort, Pocono Manor, PA 18349, telephone (800) 233-8150. Cronin's Irish Cottage is located at 1324 N. Keyser Ave. in Scranton, PA 18504, telephone (717) 342-4448.

There must be something especially compatible about Celtic celebrations and Pennsylvania's northeastern ski resorts, because the Pocono Mountain region hosts a variety of other weekend festivals to celebrate the heritage of the Irish and Scottish who settled there. Pocono's Greatest Irish Festival and the Pocono Grand Emerald Fling are both held at the Jack Frost ski resort in White Haven. Then there's the Shawnee Mountain Scottish and Irish Games and Music Festival near East Stroudsburg, and don't forget the Ancient Order of Hibernian Irish Festival at the Montage Mountain ski resort near Scranton. Each event offers authentic Celtic entertainment and food.

China

A Keystone New Year Celebration

Prior to the late 1800s, most Chinese immigrants headed west of the Rockies to work the mines and build the country's railroads. As these industries declined, Chinese-Americans became more entrepreneurial, opening small import-export businesses, garment factories, and domestic services in cities like San Francisco and Philadelphia.

With the Chinese Exclusion Act of 1882, many immigrants found themselves evicted from their homes and businesses with their rights and privileges taken away. Seeking security and moral support, many within the Chinese community retreated to Chinatowns in major cities across the United States. These Chinatowns remained isolated from mainstream America until the end of the Second World War. The country was evolving, becoming more tolerant of foreign cultures, and slowly but surely the Chinese began to move away from the cities and toward the suburbs, where they established more affluent communities described as "new" Chinatowns.

In spite of their newfound acceptance after the war, many Chinese continued to hold fast to their Asian customs and traditions. Immigrants formed their own churches, schools, newspapers, and political parties. Foods were prepared solely with Chinese ingredients using ancient methods—lucky for us!

It's easy to find Chinese ingredients and cooking equipment in groceries, hardware stores, and catalogs, because so many Americans now like to cook and eat Chinese. And it seems like there's a Chinese restaurant in every strip mall and on every block of every town in the country.

Chinese food means a lot more than chop suey and chow mein, which are considered Chinese dishes by a very loose definition only. Nowadays consumers are opting for more exotic, authentic regional cuisines and for lighter entrées in an effort to reduce dietary fat and calories.

China covers a large area, a little bigger than the United States, and it has remained regionally segregated. The country lacks the types of communication and transportation systems we enjoy here and, as a result, various regions of China developed their own unique languages and customs, including methods of food preparation. Regional cooking styles in China are often named after the large cities from which the methods originate: Szechwan, Shantung, Yangchow, Canton, Fujian, Honan, and Hunan.

In northeastern China, which includes Honan and Shantung cooking methods, dishes tend to be lighter than they are rich. Key ingredients such as leeks, scallions, chives, and garlic are found in classic dishes like Peking duck and sweet-and-sour fish.

In China's northwest, the climate is severe and growing conditions are poor. Seafood is hard to come by, as this region lies far from the coast. Salt is scarce as well, and cooks use vinegar and lemon juice to season their food. Few people from other areas of the country enjoy this type of cuisine.

In contrast to the northwest, southeastern China is agriculturally rich and has a long coastline to provide plenty of fresh seafood. Numerous styles of stir-fry cooking and other methods, including Canton, Yangchow, and Nanking, originate in the southeastern region. Typical dishes include flank steak in oyster sauce, lobster with black bean sauce, and roast pork.

Southwestern China also boasts a good agricultural base and is home for the popular Szechwan style of cooking as well as the lesser-known Kweichow and Yunnan methods. Peppery hot and spicy dishes such as Szechwan duck, pork, and shrimp originate in this region.

Historically, the majority of Chinese restaurants here in the states have used the Cantonese style of cooking. Recently, however, restaurants in metropolitan areas began to use techniques practiced in northern regions of China, and with wonderful results.

Northeastern Peking Duck

4- to 5-pound duck
6 cups water
¼ cup honey
4 slices fresh gingerroot,
⅛ inch thick each

2 green onions, sliced
12 whole green onions
Peking sauce (below)
Mandarin pancakes
(below)

Wash and pat duck dry with paper towels. Tie string tightly
around neck and suspend duck in cool, dry place for 3 hours. In
large kettle or Dutch oven, bring water to boil. Add honey, gingerroot, and sliced green onions. Lower duck by cord into boiling
water until skin is completely moistened. Hang to dry 3 more
hours. Meanwhile, cut ends from whole green onions, leaving
12 pieces, each about 4 inches long. Cut 1-inch slits in both
ends to form "brushes." Place in ice water and refrigerate until
ends curl. Remove string from duck and cut away any loose neck
skin. Place duck, breast side up, on rack over shallow roasting pan.
Roast at 375 degrees for 1 hour. Reduce heat to 300 degrees. Turn
duck on its breast and roast another 30 minutes. Increase oven
to 375 degrees and turn duck breast side up again. Roast 30 minutes
more. Transfer to carving board. Remove any crisp skin from
breast, sides, and back. Cut skin into 3×2-inch rectangles and
arrange in single layer on serving plate. Cut wings and drumsticks
from duck. Slice meat from bone and arrange on a second plate.
To serve, dip green onion "brushes" in Peking sauce and brush
on Mandarin pancakes. Lay green onion on each pancake with
a piece each of duck skin and meat. Roll pancake around meat
and onion. Eat like a sandwich. Makes 6 servings.

Peking Sauce: In small saucepan, combine ¼ cup hoisin sauce,
1 tablespoon water, 2 teaspoons sugar, and 1 teaspoon sesame oil.
Bring to boil over medium heat, stirring constantly. Reduce heat
and simmer 3 minutes, stirring constantly. Set aside to cool.

Mandarin Pancakes: Sift 2 cups all-purpose flour into large bowl.
Make well in center and pour in ¾ cup boiling water. Mix with
wooden spoon until soft dough forms. Knead on lightly floured
surface 10 minutes. Cover with damp cloth and let rest 15 minutes.
Using floured rolling pin, roll dough ¼ inch thick on lightly

Continued on next page

Mandarin Pancakes – Continued from previous page

floured surface. Using 2½-inch round biscuit cutter, cut rounds from dough, re-rolling and cutting any unused scraps. Lightly brush half of the rounds with sesame oil. Place a second, unoiled round on top of each. Using rolling pin, flatten pairs of dough to 6-inch diameter, turning once to roll both sides. Cover with dry cloth. Heat large, ungreased skillet over high heat. Reduce heat to medium. Cook pancakes one at a time in hot skillet for about 1 minute per side, turning when bubbles and brown specks appear. Gently separate halves after cooking and stack on plate.

Southeastern Bean Curd with Pork

½ pound ground pork
3 tablespoons soy sauce
2 tablespoons cornstarch
1 tablespoon hoisin sauce
1 teaspoon hot red pepper sauce
¼ teaspoon sesame oil

1 tablespoon vegetable oil
2 tablespoons chopped green onion
½ cup diced green bell pepper
4 small pieces bean curd

In medium bowl, combine pork, soy sauce, cornstarch, hoisin sauce, hot pepper sauce, and sesame oil. In wok or large skillet, heat vegetable oil over medium high heat. Add green onion. Stir-fry 1 minute. Add pork mixture, bell pepper, and bean curd. Stir-fry 10 to 15 minutes, or until pork is cooked. Serve hot. Makes 4 servings.

Northwestern Flank Steak

2-pound flank steak
¼ cup fresh lemon juice
¼ cup soy sauce

3 tablespoons honey
2 tablespoons sesame oil
3 green onions, minced

Score steak on both sides. In shallow baking dish, combine lemon juice, soy sauce, honey, oil, and green onions. Place steak in mixture, turning to coat. Cover and refrigerate several hours or overnight, turning occasionally. Transfer steak to broiler rack over shallow pan. Broil a few inches from heat about 4 minutes per side, basting occasionally with marinade from dish. Cut steak into very thin strips on an angle. Serve immediately. Makes 4 to 6 servings.

Southwestern Szechwan Shrimp

1 pound fresh shrimp, peeled
   and deveined
peanut oil for frying
2 tablespoons additional
   peanut oil
2 tablespoons minced
   green onion
2 tablespoons minced
   fresh gingerroot

2 cloves garlic, quartered
1 tablespoon catsup
1 tablespoon chili sauce
1 tablespoon dry sherry
1 tablespoon soy sauce
1 teaspoon sugar
½ teaspoon salt
¼ teaspoon dried hot
   pepper flakes

Wash and drain shrimp. In large kettle or deep-fat fryer, heat peanut oil to 375 degrees. Fry shrimp in hot oil 2 minutes. Set aside on paper-towel-lined plate to drain. In wok or large skillet, heat 2 tablespoons peanut oil over medium high heat. Add green onions, gingerroot, and garlic. Stir-fry 2 minutes, or until onions turn dark green. Remove and discard garlic. Add shrimp. Stir-fry 1 minute more. Stir in catsup, chili sauce, sherry, soy sauce, sugar, salt, and hot pepper flakes. Heat through. Serve immediately. Makes 8 servings.

A CHINESE NEW YEAR CELEBRATION

For the Chinese, the New Year is cause for their most important celebration. Chinese-Americans observe their New Year based on the lunar calendar and signs of the zodiac. Although the actual celebration always falls between the twentieth of January and February, the specific day and sign of the celebration vary from one year to the next. When my husband, Mike, and I attended New Year's dinner at the Chinese Cultural and Community Center in Philadelphia, it was the Year of the Rat.

The New Year is a time to pay off old debts and visit the head of the household with other relatives. Food, especially over several courses, is the focal point of the celebration, and we were about to sample this custom firsthand. A team of Chinese chefs from Fuzhou, Fujian, China would prepare the ten-course dinner.

The following recipes are similar to what we had that night, but not identical. The team of chefs created original recipes that were difficult to duplicate.

We began with assorted cold appetizers—sweet-and-spicy shrimp, chunks of pork and beef, sugared peanuts and pecans, tiny egg rolls, and spicy-hot slices of fresh vegetables—a nicely balanced combination of distinct flavors, textures, and colors.

Sweet-and-Spicy Shrimp

⅔ cup water
⅓ cup uncooked regular
   white rice
1 package (5 ounces) frozen
   cooked shrimp, thawed
2 green onions, sliced
1 tablespoon hoisin sauce

⅛ teaspoon dried hot
   pepper flakes
12 small leaves Bibb
   lettuce, washed
   and dried
sweet-and-sour sauce

In medium saucepan, bring water and rice to boil over medium high heat. Reduce heat to medium low. Cover and simmer 15 minutes, or until rice is tender and water absorbed. Stir in shrimp, green onions, hoisin sauce, and hot pepper flakes. Remove from heat. Spoon into bowl on center of large serving platter. Arrange lettuce leaves around bowl. To serve, spoon small amount of filling onto each lettuce leaf. Roll up and dip in sweet-and-sour sauce. Makes 12 appetizers.

Our second course was a chicken broth containing an assortment of Chinese vegetables, shiitake mushrooms, cellophane noodles, and tiny pasta. It was a soothing soup to whet the appetite and, like the first course, was not too filling.

Hot Pot

2 tablespoons dried shiitake
   mushrooms
cold water
2 tablespoons dry sherry
2 tablespoons soy sauce
salt and white pepper, to taste
pinch ground ginger
½ pound boneless pork,
   cut in thin strips
1 quart lightly salted water
½ pound transparent noodles

2 quarts (8 cups)
   chicken broth
2 cups sliced bamboo
   shoots
2 tablespoons vegetable
   oil
1 cup diced cooked
   chicken
1 cup diced cooked ham
½ cup chopped fresh
   watercress

In small bowl, cover mushrooms with cold water. Soak 30 minutes. Drain, slice, and set aside. In medium bowl, combine sherry, soy sauce, salt, pepper, and ginger. Add pork and toss to coat. Cover and let stand 1 hour. In large kettle or Dutch oven, bring lightly salted water to boil. Add noodles. Cook 10 minutes. Drain and set aside. Place chicken broth in large kettle or Dutch oven. Bring to boil. Add mushrooms, bamboo shoots, and noodles. Reduce heat and simmer 2 minutes. Remove pork from soy sauce mixture. Pat dry. In large skillet, heat oil over medium high heat. Add pork and sauté 2 minutes. Add pork, chicken, ham, and watercress to chicken broth. Heat through. Spoon into bowls. Makes 6 servings.

Our third course consisted of pounded, chopped chicken balls lightly coated in rice flour and fried. These little meatballs were mildly seasoned and tasted great dipped in soy sauce. They were served with steamed white rice.

Chicken Balls with Oyster Sauce

2 boneless, skinless whole chicken breasts, chopped
2 green onions, chopped
2 tablespoons water
1 tablespoon dry sherry
1 tablespoon cornstarch
1 teaspoon salt
vegetable oil
½ cup finely chopped onions

¼ cup chicken broth
2 tablespoons oyster sauce
1 teaspoon sugar
½ teaspoon freshly grated gingerroot
salt and coarsely ground black pepper, to taste

Place chicken in food processor and chop fine. Add green onions, water, sherry, cornstarch, and 1 teaspoon salt. Shape into small balls about ½ inch wide. In large skillet, heat thin coating of vegetable oil over medium high heat. Add chicken balls. Fry until browned on all sides. Pour off excess oil. Reduce heat to low. Add onions, chicken broth, oyster sauce, sugar, and gingerroot. Cook and stir 5 minutes. Salt and pepper to taste. Serve hot. Makes 4 servings.

For course four, we had juicy jumbo shrimp stir-fried with mushrooms and Chinese vegetables. This course was very tasty and wasn't too filling for us to have seconds.

Shrimp Stir-Fry

vegetable oil
1 cup diagonally sliced celery
1 cup sliced fresh mushrooms
½ cup sliced green onions
½ pound cooked jumbo shrimp,
    peeled and deveined

½ pound fresh bean
    sprouts
soy sauce

In wok or large skillet, heat oil over medium high heat. Add celery. Stir-fry until bright green. Add mushrooms and green onions. Stir-fry 1 minute. Add shrimp and bean sprouts. Toss 2 minutes, or just until heated through. Sprinkle with soy sauce. Serve immediately. Makes 2 to 3 servings.

For course five, strips of lean beef were stir-fried with fresh, sweet snow peas and served in a spicy-hot sauce that went well over the steamed rice.

Beef with Snow Peas

marinade (below)
½ pound lean beef, thinly sliced
2 teaspoons cornstarch
2 teaspoons cold water
½ teaspoon sugar
⅛ teaspoon coarsely ground
   black pepper
2 tablespoons vegetable oil,
   divided

½ pound fresh snow peas,
   trimmed
1 teaspoon freshly grated
   gingerroot
¼ teaspoon salt
½ cup chicken broth

Place beef in marinade, turning to coat. Cover and refrigerate several hours or overnight. Thoroughly combine cornstarch and cold water. Stir in sugar and pepper. In wok or large skillet, heat 1 tablespoon of the oil over medium high heat. Add snow peas, gingerroot, and salt. Stir-fry 1 to 2 minutes. Add chicken broth. Heat through, and remove from wok. Add remaining 1 table-spoon oil to wok. Heat over medium high heat. Remove beef from marinade and add to wok. Stir-fry 1 minute. Add snow peas and cornstarch mixture. Stir until sauce is thickened. Serve immediately. Makes 2 to 3 servings.

Marinade: In shallow dish, combine 2 teaspoons dry sherry, 1 teaspoon cornstarch, 1 teaspoon soy sauce, ¼ teaspoon sugar, and ¼ teaspoon vegetable oil.

Course six was my favorite: boneless, lean pork spareribs cooked in a spicy barbecue sauce.

Spareribs in Honey Sauce

3 pounds lean pork spareribs, cut into individual ribs
salt and coarsely ground black pepper, to taste
3 tablespoons vegetable oil
1 medium onion, finely chopped
1 clove garlic, crushed

1 cup chicken broth
¼ cup orange juice
¼ cup soy sauce
2 tablespoons fresh lemon juice
2 tablespoons honey
1 tablespoon prepared mustard

Arrange ribs in roasting pan. Sprinkle with salt and pepper. Set aside. In medium saucepan, heat oil over medium high heat. Add onion and garlic. Sauté 3 to 4 minutes, or just until onions are soft. Whisk in chicken broth, orange juice, soy sauce, lemon juice, honey, and mustard. Bring to boil. Pour hot mixture over spareribs in pan. Bake at 325 degrees for 1½ hours, basting frequently. Remove from pan and serve hot. Makes 4 to 6 servings.

For the seventh course, lean, succulent pieces of roast duckling seasoned with a mild orange sauce were served with broccoli rabe.

Chinese Duck with Orange Sauce

2 cups dry sherry
3- to 4-pound duck, cut up
salt, to taste
½ cup honey
2 tablespoons soy sauce
2 tablespoons finely chopped
  candied ginger

2 teaspoons dry mustard
1 teaspoon sesame seeds
2 tablespoons butter
orange sauce (below)
orange slices
fresh parsley

Arrange duck in large shallow bowl. Sprinkle with salt. In small bowl, whisk together honey, soy sauce, ginger, mustard, and sesame seeds. Pour over duck. Cover and refrigerate 3 hours, turning duck occasionally. Remove duck from bowl, reserving marinade. Drain duck on paper towels. In large skillet, melt butter over medium high heat. Add duck and brown well on all sides. Transfer to baking pan. Bake at 350 degrees for 1 hour and 10 minutes, basting occasionally with reserved marinade. Place on large serving platter. Garnish with orange slices, parsley, and mandarin orange segments and banana slices left over from sauce recipe. Serve orange sauce in separate bowl. Makes 4 servings.

Orange Sauce: Peel ½ of a medium orange and cut rind into thin strips. Squeeze juice from 6 oranges. In small saucepan, combine orange juice, rind, and 1 tablespoon finely chopped candied ginger. Stir in 3 tablespoons sugar and 2 tablespoons dry sherry. Whisk over medium heat until hot. Thoroughly combine 2 tablespoons additional sherry and 1 teaspoon cornstarch. Gradually add to orange juice mixture, whisking constantly. Cook and whisk until thick and bubbly. Remove from heat. Drain juice from one 11-ounce can mandarin orange segments. Add half of the mandarin oranges to the orange juice mixture. Stir in ½ sliced banana. Serve sauce warm, garnishing duck with remaining half of mandarin orange segments and banana slices.

Course eight, stir-fried green vegetables, was a nice change of pace from the spicy meats and sweet sauces. The mixture we had contained just a bit of sausage for flavor.

Stir-Fried Broccoli with Sesame Seeds

1 medium bunch fresh broccoli, washed and trimmed
½ cup vegetable broth
1 tablespoon rice wine
2 teaspoons soy sauce
¼ teaspoon salt
3 tablespoons peanut oil

1 teaspoon grated fresh ginger
2 tablespoons lightly toasted sesame seeds (see note)
1 teaspoon sesame oil

Cut broccoli into small florets and cut stems into ½-inch slices. Set aside. In small bowl, combine vegetable broth, wine, soy sauce, and salt. Set aside. In wok or large skillet, heat peanut oil over medium high heat. Add ginger. Stir-fry 15 seconds. Add broccoli and vegetable broth mixture. Cover and cook 3 minutes. Sprinkle with sesame seeds. Drizzle with sesame oil. Serve immediately. Makes 4 to 6 servings.

Note: To toast sesame seeds, place in dry skillet. Cook over medium low heat 3 minutes, or until lightly browned and fragrant, shaking pan constantly while cooking.

At a Chinese New Year banquet, whole fish is always served just before dessert to symbolize abundance. The fish was tender and tasty and was served with a sweet orange sauce and fried dumplings.

Steamed Whole Fish

1½ pounds whole flounder, trout, sea bass, or pike, scaled and cleaned
1 teaspoon salt
½ teaspoon coarsely ground black pepper
¼ teaspoon ground ginger
3 cups water

2 tablespoons minced green onions
2 teaspoons mixed pickling spice
2 bay leaves
2 cloves garlic, halved
lemon slices
fresh parsley

Lightly score flesh of fish. In small bowl, combine salt, pepper, and ginger. Rub onto fish. Set aside. In wok or large skillet, combine water, green onions, pickling spice, bay leaves, and garlic. Bring to a simmer. Place steaming rack over top. Place fish on rack. Cover and steam over simmering water 30 minutes, or until tender and flaky. Place on serving platter. Garnish with lemon slices and parsley. Makes 3 to 4 servings.

The tenth course was our dessert—small date logs rolled in toasted sesame seeds—a not-too-sweet ending to a wonderful meal.

Sesame-Date Confections

2 cups finely chopped dates
½ cup water
¼ cup honey
1½ cups shredded coconut

1 cup finely chopped pecans
½ teaspoon vanilla extract
1 cup toasted sesame seeds
   (see note)

In large, heavy saucepan, combine dates, water, and honey. Cook over low heat 5 minutes or until thickened, stirring constantly. Remove from heat. Stir in coconut, pecans, and vanilla extract. Set aside at room temperature until cool enough to handle. Shape into 1-inch balls and roll in sesame seeds. Cool completely on waxed-paper-lined tray. Serve at room temperature. Store in tightly sealed container in refrigerator. (May be frozen.) Makes about 3 dozen.
   Note: To toast sesame seeds, place in dry skillet. Cook over medium low heat 3 minutes, or until lightly browned and fragrant, shaking pan constantly while cooking. Cool.

The Chinese Cultural and Community Center schedules its Chinese New Year banquets Tuesday through Sunday evenings, mid-February through early spring. The cost per person is $25 to $28. Advance reservations are required. To make reservations or for additional information, call (215) 923-6767 or 6768.

If you'd like to try your hand at Chinese cooking, there are dozens of good cookbooks to get you started. I like *The Pleasures of Chinese Cooking*, by Grace Zia Chu (Cornerstone Library Publications, 1973), and *Classic Chinese Cooking for the Vegetarian Gourmet*, by Joanne Hush (Smallwood & Stewart, 1984). Both books are user-friendly and practical for contemporary kitchens.

India

Culinary Traditions from the Homeland

The peninsula of India is the most populous country in South Asia and is second in population only to China. About 900 million people of widely diverse ethnicity, religions, and languages (including hundreds of dialects) live in India and, as a result, there is an impressive variety of food customs.

The Indian community here in the States is just as ethnically diverse, and various subgroups can trace their roots to different states or regions within India. The largest Indian subgroups in the United States are Bengalis, Gujaratis, Punjabis, Marathis, and Tamils. About a third live in the northeastern states, including Pennsylvania, and most perpetuate the food traditions and celebrations specific to their heritage.

Just about all Indian recipes are made with some combination of common spices such as turmeric, cumin, cardamom, ginger, chili powder, cinnamon, and cloves. More unusual spices like black onion seeds, called kalonji (or kala jeera), are also used extensively, and recipes may call for as many as fifteen spices to create flavors ranging from subtle to hot, hotter, and hottest. Sometimes spices are used whole in cooking, then removed just before the dish is served. Just as often, the spice is freshly ground for optimum flavor and blended into the food before it is cooked.

Asian Indians have understood the health attributes of beans, rice, and vegetables for centuries. They enjoy spicy lentil dishes and seemingly unlimited combinations of chaval (rice), beans, and fresh vegetables. Everyday vegetables such as carrots, green beans, and cauliflower are prepared "dry," or without a sauce, but for festive occasions, vegetables are served "wet," dressed in spicy sauces and presented to guests in individual serving bowls.

Popular recipes in southern India include masala, which are crepes filled with spicy potatoes, and idlis, or steamed rice cakes. Tandoori, a clay-baked chicken marinated in yogurt, and a flavored rice with vegetables and meat called biryani are popular among Indians from northern regions. Hindus, the largest religious group among Indians, will not eat beef, and Muslims refuse pork, although second-generation Hindus and Muslims are more inclined to ignore such religious taboos. Most Indians enjoy unleavened and leavened breads, as well as chutney, spicy fritters, and pickled vegetables.

Traditional Indian cooking can be time-consuming, since recipes are prepared from scratch and usually call for fresh ingredients. Indian-

Americans do use shortcuts, however, relying on more processed, ready-to-use substitutes such as canned beans and seasoning blends so readily available in this country. More unusual ingredients are purchased at specialty gourmet shops and Indian markets.

If you'd like to try your hand at some Indian dishes in your own kitchen, consider one of the following cookbooks to get you started. Madhur Jaffrey's *Indian Cooking* (Barron's Educational Series, 1983) contains wonderful background information as well as recipes. For easy-to-follow instruction, I like the step-by-step format of *Quick & Easy Indian Cooking*, by Louise Steele, and *Indian Side Dishes*, by Cara Hobday (both published by Shooting Star Press, 1995).

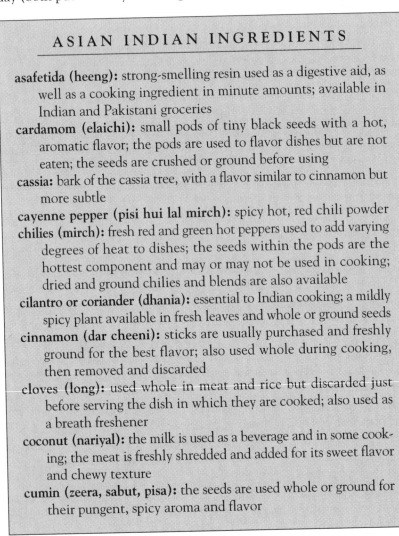

ASIAN INDIAN INGREDIENTS

asafetida (heeng): strong-smelling resin used as a digestive aid, as well as a cooking ingredient in minute amounts; available in Indian and Pakistani groceries

cardamom (elaichi): small pods of tiny black seeds with a hot, aromatic flavor; the pods are used to flavor dishes but are not eaten; the seeds are crushed or ground before using

cassia: bark of the cassia tree, with a flavor similar to cinnamon but more subtle

cayenne pepper (pisi hui lal mirch): spicy hot, red chili powder

chilies (mirch): fresh red and green hot peppers used to add varying degrees of heat to dishes; the seeds within the pods are the hottest component and may or may not be used in cooking; dried and ground chilies and blends are also available

cilantro or coriander (dhania): essential to Indian cooking; a mildly spicy plant available in fresh leaves and whole or ground seeds

cinnamon (dar cheeni): sticks are usually purchased and freshly ground for the best flavor; also used whole during cooking, then removed and discarded

cloves (long): used whole in meat and rice but discarded just before serving the dish in which they are cooked; also used as a breath freshener

coconut (nariyal): the milk is used as a beverage and in some cooking; the meat is freshly shredded and added for its sweet flavor and chewy texture

cumin (zeera, sabut, pisa): the seeds are used whole or ground for their pungent, spicy aroma and flavor

curry powder: a blend of savory and hot spices used extensively in Indian dishes

fennel seeds (sonf): sweet, anise-flavored seeds often presented at the end of a meal to aid digestion and freshen breath

fenugreek (methi): dull, mustard-colored seeds with a bitter taste when ground

garam masala: a ground mix of spices that usually includes cardamom, cinnamon, cloves, cumin, nutmeg, and pepper; used sparingly to season meats and vegetables

ghee: clarified butter, which can be homemade or purchased in cans at Asian Indian food stores; gives dishes a rich, nutty flavor; vegetable oil is a less flavorful substitute

ginger (adrak): fresh root with a pungent flavor and potatolike texture; it is sliced, grated, chopped, or mashed into a paste to flavor many foods

gram flour: garbanzo bean flour used as a thickener and coating for deep-fat frying; available in Asian Indian stores

mustard oil (sarson ka tel): excellent, pungent flavoring for cooking vegetables and fish; must be heated to bring out its uniquely sweet aroma; available in Indian stores; rapeseed oil is a less desirable substitute

mustard seeds (sarson): tiny, round, reddish brown seeds used to season many dishes, including vegetables and salads

nigella (kalonji): small, black, tear-shaped seed with a nutty aroma used for pickling, fish and vegetable recipes, and on bread

nutmeg (jaiphal): used whole in simmering dishes for its nutty flavor; removed and discarded before the dish is served

saffron (zaafraan, kesar): an expensive spice with a distinctive flavor and aroma; contributes yellow coloring to many dishes; available as a powder or in threadlike strands

sesame seeds (til): usually roasted to enhance their nutty flavor; used in a variety of recipes

turmeric (haldi): mild, earthy-tasting root that is dried and ground to a bright orange powder; gives many Indian foods their yellow color; also used as a digestive aid and antiseptic

vark: fragile, silvery tissue used to garnish sweets and holiday dishes; available in Indian and Pakistani grocery stores

yogurt (dahi): cultured milk product used to marinate meat and poultry and as an ingredient for sauces and drinks

Custom Curry Powder

2 dried red chili peppers
2 teaspoons cumin seeds
2 teaspoons coriander seeds
1 teaspoon cardamom seeds
1 teaspoon yellow mustard seeds

1 teaspoon ground
   turmeric
½ teaspoon ground ginger
6 whole cloves
2-inch cinnamon stick

In skillet, heat all ingredients over medium low heat, stirring constantly, until very lightly browned and aromatic. Cool to room temperature. Using a spice or coffee grinder, grind to a fine powder. Store in a tightly sealed glass jar away from heat and light.

Garam Masala

1 tablespoon cardamom seeds
1 small cinnamon stick
1 teaspoon black peppercorns

1 teaspoon cumin seeds
1 teaspoon whole cloves
¼ medium nutmeg

Using a spice or coffee grinder, grind all ingredients to a fine powder. Store in a tightly sealed jar away from heat and light.

Ghee

Cut 1 pound sweet (unsalted) butter into small pieces. Place in heavy saucepan. Melt slowly over medium low heat, stirring constantly (do not brown). Increase heat to medium high and bring to a boil. When surface is completely covered with foam, stir butter and quickly reduce heat to lowest temperature. Simmer, uncovered and without stirring, 45 minutes or until solids on bottom of pan are golden brown and liquid on top is transparent. Slowly pour transparent butter (ghee) through strainer lined with 4 layers of dampened cheesecloth into large bowl. (If any solids remain in ghee, repeat straining until completely clear.) Pour ghee into glass jar. Seal tightly and store in refrigerator or at room temperature until ready to use. Ghee will solidify when refrigerated. When ready to use, melt over very low heat but do not allow to brown. May be stored up to 3 months. Makes about 1½ cups.

Didar Singh is proud of his award-winning, Pittsburgh-based restaurant, the India Garden. Singh, born in Penjab, not only owns the India Garden, but is also its head chef and a purist when it comes to preparing authentic recipes from the northern regions of India. For example, you won't find an electric oven or stove in Singh's restaurant kitchen. Instead, two vat-shaped clay ovens called *tandoors*, which Singh had shipped from India, are heated to impressive temperatures with charcoal and used exclusively for cooking and baking. Tandoors impart a wonderful flavor to Indian foods that's difficult to duplicate using other methods.

It's no surprise, then, to learn that tandoori chicken and shrimp dishes are popular at the India Garden. So are fresh vegetables, like peas with cheese, okra, and eggplant. Singh uses low-cholesterol cooking techniques without sacrificing the wonderful, spicy-fresh aroma and flavor so characteristic of classic Indian cuisine.

You'll find plenty of lamb, seafood, and curry dishes on the India Garden menu. For example, there's biryani. Singh's version includes succulent lamb, seafood, rice, and vegetables seasoned with cumin, cinnamon, cloves, and black pepper.

The India Garden desserts are in a class of their own, too. Kulfi, a classic Indian ice cream, is made from reduced milk (instead of heavy cream) spiced with cardamom, then flavored with pistachio before freezing. A rice pudding called kheer is made with basmati rice and a thickened milk sauce and is similar to the classic rice pudding many of us make.

The India Garden is somewhat upscale, and reservations are requested, especially on weekends. The restaurant is located at 328 Atwood St. in Pittsburgh. For reservations, call (412) 682-3000.

Tandoori Murghi
(Tandoori-Style Chicken)

6 boneless, skinless chicken breast halves
1¼ teaspoons salt
1 cup plain yogurt
3 tablespoons fresh lemon juice
2 cloves garlic, minced
1¾ teaspoons garam masala (see page 118)
1¼ teaspoons ground ginger
¼ teaspoon cayenne (ground red pepper)
1 tablespoon olive oil
2 cups halved and thinly sliced onions
lemon wedges

Using a sharp knife, make diagonal slashes at 1-inch intervals in skinned side of each chicken breast. Sprinkle with salt. Set aside. In shallow bowl, combine yogurt, lemon juice, garlic, garam masala, ginger, and cayenne. Add chicken breasts, turning to coat with mixture. Cover and refrigerate several hours or overnight. Lightly brush 13×9-inch oblong baking dish with about 1 teaspoon of the olive oil. Remove chicken from yogurt mixture and arrange in dish, slashed sides up. Spoon small amount of marinade over top, discarding remainder. Sprinkle with onions. Drizzle with remaining olive oil. Bake at 375 degrees for 25 to 30 minutes, or until tender and cooked through. Broil a few inches from heat 3 minutes or just until onions begin to brown. Serve immediately with lemon wedges. Makes 6 servings.

Kulfi (Indian Ice Cream)

5 tablespoons boiling water
4 cardamom pods, crushed
   and seeds removed
1 can (14 ounces) sweetened
   condensed milk
5 tablespoons cold water
¼ cup unsalted pistachio
   nuts

¼ cup almonds
⅔ cup heavy or whipping
   cream
additional pistachio nuts
   or almonds

In small bowl, pour boiling water over cardamom pods. Let stand 15 minutes. Strain and cool water. Meanwhile, in blender or food processor, combine condensed milk, cold water, pistachio nuts, and almonds. Process 30 seconds or until finely ground. Transfer to medium bowl. Add cooled cardamom water, mixing well. Set aside. In cold bowl, whip cream until soft peaks form. Fold into nut mixture. Pour into shallow metal pan or plastic container. Cover tightly and freeze 3 hours, or until partially frozen. Transfer to bowl. Mash with fork and divide among individual serving cups or molds. Cover and freeze several hours or overnight. To unmold, quickly dip base of each cup or mold in hot water and run knife around edge to loosen. Invert onto serving plates. Garnish with additional pistachios or almonds. Serve immediately. Makes 6 to 8 servings.

My research on Pennsylvania-based Asian Indian events began at the Kingston Armory near Wilkes-Barre. It was October, and the armory was hosting its last-ever multicultural festival. That's where I met Neelam Jain, a pretty Indian girl who smiled graciously as she served up savory treats from her homeland. Neelam talked about the Hindu "festival of light" called Divali.

I found out that Divali is the most celebrated of all Indian holidays, usually between mid-October and mid-November. This cultural and religious rite marks the beginning of the Hindu new year with a line of oil lamps, lit to signify hopes for a smooth life and the triumph of good (or light) over evil (darkness). Children set off firecrackers, homes are spruced up to symbolize a fresh start, and special foods are prepared for the occasion. Giving sweets to family, friends, and colleagues is an integral part of the Divali tradition, and the variety of recipes for these candylike gifts seems endless. There are dozens of regional and community specialties presented to guests on ornate platters, much as many of us would offer holiday cookies to yuletide visitors.

I had read a story in the local newspaper about a Divali celebration at the Hindu temple in New Cumberland, and I spoke with Naelima Parikh, who helped to coordinate the New Cumberland Divali celebration, about some typical Divali sweets. She told me that almond cookies called badam puri are usually served, along with a cashew nut candy called kaju katri. Chum chum, a candy make from the curds of cooked condensed milk, is popular, as is birani, sweetened saffron rice.

I also asked Naelima about the foods served at New Cumberland's Divali celebration. Savory dishes offered there included an assortment of spicy rice pilafs and mixed vegetables seasoned with ginger and garlic. There was a creamy soup called kadhi, flavored with cumin, coriander, and chili peppers, and the popular leavened bread, naan. Many of the appetizers were baked or deep-fried. Potato puffs were made from seasoned mashed potatoes rolled in chick pea flour and fried to a crisp, golden brown. Papad was a baked wafer usually eaten with rice.

The Indian community, with some donations from area Indian restaurants, prepares the fifty to sixty dishes served to about 500 people at the New Cumberland Divali. It is open to the public for just $1, and the temple welcomes donations. For more information, call the Hindu American Religious Institute in New Cumberland at (717) 774-7750.

Naan (Leavened Bread)

⅔ cup warm (not hot) milk
2 teaspoons active dry yeast
2 teaspoons sugar, divided
3¼ cups unbleached
   all-purpose flour

1 teaspoon baking powder
½ teaspoon salt
⅔ cup plain yogurt
2 tablespoons vegetable oil
1 egg, slightly beaten

Place warm milk in small bowl. Stir in yeast and 1 teaspoon of the sugar. Let stand 15 minutes. In large bowl, combine flour, baking powder, salt, and remaining 1 teaspoon sugar. Stir in yeast mixture, yogurt, oil, and egg. Continue stirring until soft dough forms. Turn out onto lightly floured surface. Knead 10 to 15 minutes, or until dough is smooth and elastic. Form into ball. Lightly oil clean bowl. Add dough, turning to coat with oil. Cover loosely with plastic wrap or damp cloth. Let rise in warm place 1 hour or until doubled in volume. Preheat oven to 500 degrees or highest temperature (to simulate the hot tandoor oven). Place a heavy baking sheet in oven. Punch down dough and knead on floured surface a few minutes. Divide into six equal portions. Keeping remaining portions covered with a damp cloth, roll out one portion on lightly floured surface to form large, flat oval. Slap onto hot baking sheet in oven. Bake 3 minutes or until puffy. Broil a few inches from heat about 30 seconds, or until top is lightly browned. Wrap in clean cloth towel. Repeat shaping, baking, and grilling procedure with remaining dough. Serve warm. Makes 6 loaves.

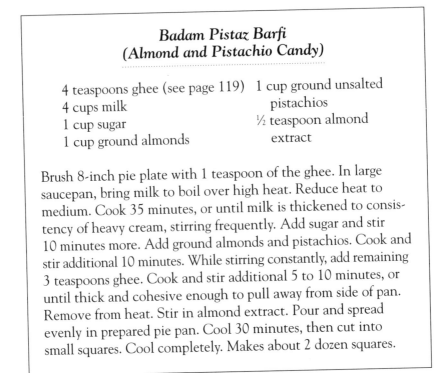

Badam Pistaz Barfi
(Almond and Pistachio Candy)

4 teaspoons ghee (see page 119)   1 cup ground unsalted
4 cups milk   pistachios
1 cup sugar   ½ teaspoon almond
1 cup ground almonds   extract

Brush 8-inch pie plate with 1 teaspoon of the ghee. In large saucepan, bring milk to boil over high heat. Reduce heat to medium. Cook 35 minutes, or until milk is thickened to consistency of heavy cream, stirring frequently. Add sugar and stir 10 minutes more. Add ground almonds and pistachios. Cook and stir additional 10 minutes. While stirring constantly, add remaining 3 teaspoons ghee. Cook and stir additional 5 to 10 minutes, or until thick and cohesive enough to pull away from side of pan. Remove from heat. Stir in almond extract. Pour and spread evenly in prepared pie pan. Cool 30 minutes, then cut into small squares. Cool completely. Makes about 2 dozen squares.

When I entered the Divali celebration at Wilkes University in Wilkes-Barre, I saw women and children dressed in the vibrant red, purple, and embroidered silk, taffeta, and chiffon representative of their Indian heritage. Mothers and daughters wore matching headpieces woven into their long, dark hair with rich, gold jewelry accents. The men wore traditional American suits.

Like other Divali celebrations and many American holidays, this one was very upbeat and focused on family, especially children. As many as four generations were represented there. The children danced and bounced with knobbed sticks while a young boy played classic Indian music on a keyboard. It was easy to pick out proud parents and grandparents as they looked on with video cameras and broad smiles.

Toward the end of the night, we ate from a long, colorful buffet of vegetarian foods. Each year one Indian restaurant from the area is invited to cater the event, and this time the beautiful feast was prepared by an Allentown restaurant called Star of India.

There was a spicy, yellow lentil soup called dal (sometimes presented as a side dish), a vegetable rice pilaf (pilau), and a nicely seasoned, not-too-spicy potato and cauliflower side dish called alu gobi. Spiced chick peas called chana masala were popular and went well with naan. I tried not to fill up on samosa, a vegetable-filled pastry, and ate just small dabs of tomato and mint chutneys so I would have room for gulab jamun, a dessert pastry topped with honey syrup.

The Wilkes-Barre Divali festival serves up plenty of food and entertainment for $12 per adult and $2 to $6 per child. Advance reservations are requested. For more information, call (717) 825-5510 or write the Indo-American Association of Northeast Pennsylvania, P.O. Box 2380, Wilkes-Barre, PA 18702.

Similar Divali celebrations are held throughout the state. For more information, contact the Hindu temple in cities such as Pittsburgh, Allentown, and Williamsport.

Dal

⅓ cup yellow split peas
cold water
5 cups water
½ teaspoon turmeric
1 onion, chopped
1 teaspoon ground cumin
2 tablespoons vegetable oil
½ teaspoon mustard seeds

2 cloves garlic, crushed
2 dried chilies, seeded
    and chopped
1 cup canned chopped
    tomatoes
salt and coarsely ground
    black peppercorns,
    to taste

Soak split peas in cold water, refrigerated overnight. Drain and rinse. Place in large saucepan with 5 cups water and turmeric. Bring to boil. Reduce heat and cover. Simmer 30 minutes. Stir in onion and cumin. Cover and cook 15 minutes more. In skillet, heat oil over medium heat. Add mustard seeds. Stir until popped. Add garlic, chilies, and tomatoes. Cook and stir 2 to 3 minutes. Add to lentil mixture. Salt and pepper to taste. Adjust liquid as desired to serve as a soup or side dish. Makes 4 to 6 servings.

Rice Pilau (Pilaf)

3 tablespoons vegetable oil
1 onion, halved and
   thinly sliced
3 shallots, minced
2 cups basmati rice, uncooked
1 clove garlic, crushed
1 teaspoon freshly grated
   gingerroot
½ teaspoon cayenne
   (ground red pepper)

4 cups chicken broth
1 teaspoon crushed saffron
¼ teaspoon orange zest
2 cups frozen peas, thawed
⅓ cup golden raisins
1 tablespoon fresh lemon
   juice
snipped fresh cilantro

In large skillet, heat oil over medium high heat. Add onion.
Sauté until lightly browned. Remove from skillet and drain on
paper towels. Reduce heat to medium. To oil in same skillet, add
shallots. Sauté 5 minutes, or until soft. Stir in rice, garlic, gingerroot, and cayenne. Add chicken broth, saffron, and orange zest.
Bring to boil. Simmer 15 minutes. Add peas, raisins, and lemon
juice, mixing well. Garnish with fresh cilantro. Serve immediately.
Makes 6 servings.

The Pennsylvania Renaissance Faire has gained quite a following among
fans of sixteenth-century English history and lore. Amid the lifelike jousting
of armored knights, visitors walk the streets of a Tudor village, while fully
costumed Shakespearean actors talk the talk of merry old England. You
might wonder what this discussion is doing in the middle of a chapter on
Indian cuisine. It's not as strange as you might think, since the Renaissance
Faire features an Asian Indian celebration during its eleven-weekend run.

Vishnu Shenoy owns and operates A Passage to India, a popular
restaurant in Harrisburg that has catered the Renaissance Faire's event
in past years. He told me that tandoori chicken and curried meat dishes
were very popular at the Faire. He described vegetable korma, a blend
of fresh vegetables in a creamy almond sauce, and vegetable samosa, a
light, crisp pastry stuffed with cumin-seasoned mashed potatoes, peas,
and cashews, then deep-fried and served with chutney—quite a journey
from hot dogs and caramel corn.

A Passage to India has served generous platters, ranging from just
$2.95 to $4.95, to more than 200 people at the Renaissance Faire. If

you can't make it to Mount Hope in time for the Faire's Asian Indian weekend, then at least call A Passage to India at (717) 233-1202 for reservations.

In more recent years, The Great Life Cafe, located in Annville, Pennsylvania, has catered the Renaissance Faire's Indian weekend. Great Life has taken a more casual approach to feeding hungry fairgoers by offering vegetarian hummus and couscous platters for about $4.

The Pennsylvania Renaissance Faire is located on Route 72, just off Exit 20 of the Pennsylvania Turnpike. The Faire runs weekends from August through mid-October. Admission is $15.95 for adults and $7 for children. For more information, call (717) 665-7021.

Hummus

Hummus is an interesting dish. I tried my first variations of this garbanzo bean filling or dip a few years ago. I was developing a new product prototype for an organic food company, trying to get just the right combination of garbanzos, tahini, and garlic. I must have gone through a case of chick peas and smelled like fresh garlic for weeks. (Fortunately, my husband loves garlic.)

½ cup dry chick peas
   (garbanzo beans)
½ cup tahini (sesame butter)
3 tablespoons fresh lemon juice
2 cloves garlic

dash cayenne (ground
   red pepper)
salt and coarsely ground
   black pepper, to taste

Cover chick peas with water. Cover and refrigerate overnight to soak. Drain and place soaked beans in medium saucepan, and cover with fresh water. Bring to boil. Reduce heat. Cover and simmer 2 hours or until very tender. Drain, reserving cooking water. Transfer beans to food processor. With processor running, add just enough cooking water through chute to form desired spreading or dipping consistency. Add tahini, lemon juice, garlic, and cayenne. Process until smooth. Salt and pepper to taste. Use as a pita filling, dip, or spread. Makes about 2 cups.

Couscous

Couscous is one of those dishes with many variations around the world. The original couscous grain is actually the bulgur of North Africa, where it is generally served with pieces of meat or vegetables. In India, couscous is spiced with curry or cumin and served as a vegetarian main dish. Millet, bulgur, and barley are fine substitutes for couscous in the recipes here. In smaller amounts, it's a fine side dish, too.

4 cups water
2 teaspoons salt, divided
1 cup couscous, bulgur, millet, or barley
2 tablespoons butter
1 tablespoon minced fresh, hot red chili pepper
4 cups coarsely chopped yellow summer squash
½ medium cauliflower, cut into small florets

2 large carrots, sliced thick
1 large onion, halved and thinly sliced
4 cups diced fresh tomatoes
2 cups canned chick peas (garbanzo beans), drained
spicy cumin sauce (below)

In large kettle, bring water to a boil. Add 1 teaspoon of the salt. Stir in couscous, bulgur, millet, or barley. Reduce heat and simmer 20 minutes. Strain through fine sieve. Stir in butter and chili pepper. Layer cooked grain in steamer with squash, cauliflower, carrots, and onion. Steam 20 to 30 minutes, or until vegetables are tender. Meanwhile, combine tomatoes and remaining 1 teaspoon salt in medium saucepan. Cook and stir over medium low heat 10 minutes, or until tomatoes are tender. Stir in chick peas and heat through, stirring occasionally. Arrange couscous and steamed vegetables on serving platter. Top with tomato mixture. Serve immediately with spicy cumin sauce. Makes 4 to 6 servings.

Spicy Cumin Sauce: In medium bowl, combine 2 peeled and finely chopped tomatoes, ¼ cup snipped fresh parsley, 1 tablespoon extra-virgin olive oil, 2 minced green onions, 1 minced clove garlic, ½ teaspoon cumin, ½ teaspoon dried hot pepper flakes, and ¼ teaspoon salt. Let stand at room temperature a few hours to blend flavors. Cover and refrigerate until ready to serve.

Chicken Curry

2 tablespoons olive oil
6 boneless, skinless chicken
   breasts, cubed
3 tablespoons sweet
   (unsalted) butter
1 medium onion, chopped
2 cloves garlic, crushed
1 tart apple, diced
1 green bell pepper, diced
1 small jalapeño pepper, minced

2 tablespoons curry
   powder
¼ cup all-purpose flour
1½ cups chicken broth
salt and coarsely ground
   black peppercorns,
   to taste
rice pilaf
fresh cilantro

In large skillet, heat olive oil over medium heat. Add chicken. Sauté 12 minutes, or until brown on all sides. Remove from skillet and set aside. In same skillet, melt butter over medium heat. Add onion and garlic. Sauté 6 minutes, or until lightly browned. Return chicken to skillet. Add apple, bell pepper, jalapeño pepper, curry powder, and flour. Cook and stir 5 minutes. Whisk in chicken broth. Simmer 20 minutes, stirring occasionally. Salt and pepper to taste. Spoon over hot rice pilaf. Garnish with fresh cilantro. Serve immediately. Makes 8 servings.

Phool Gobi Aur Aloo Ki Bhaji
(Cauliflower with Potatoes)

1 small head cauliflower, trimmed and cut into small florets
2 medium potatoes with skins
⅓ cup vegetable oil
1 teaspoon whole cumin seeds
1 small jalapeño pepper, minced
1 teaspoon ground cumin
½ teaspoon ground roasted cumin seeds (see note)
½ teaspoon ground coriander
¼ teaspoon ground turmeric
⅛ teaspoon cayenne (ground red pepper)
salt and coarsely ground black peppercorns, to taste

Soak cauliflower in cold water 30 minutes. Meanwhile, in medium saucepan, cover unpeeled potatoes with cold water. Bring to boil. Reduce heat to medium. Cover and cook 20 minutes, or until fork tender. Drain and cool completely. Peel and dice. Set aside. In large skillet, heat oil over medium heat. Add whole cumin seeds. Sauté 3 to 4 minutes. Drain cauliflower and add to sautéed cumin seeds. Sauté 2 minutes, or until lightly browned. Reduce heat to low and cover. Simmer 5 minutes, or until cauliflower is crisp-tender. Add diced potatoes, jalapeño pepper, ground cumin, roasted cumin, coriander, turmeric, and cayenne, mixing well. Salt and pepper to taste. Cook uncovered over low heat, stirring constantly, for 3 minutes, or until heated through. Makes 4 to 6 servings.

Note: To roast cumin seeds, place whole seeds in a heavy skillet over medium heat. Stir constantly until darkened. Grind.

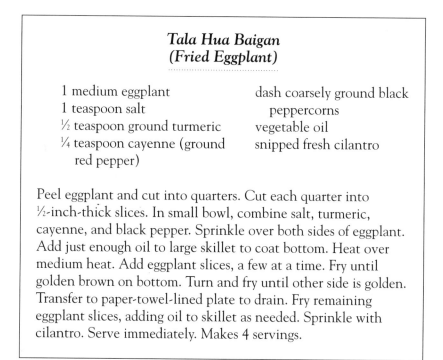

Tala Hua Baigan
(Fried Eggplant)

1 medium eggplant
1 teaspoon salt
½ teaspoon ground turmeric
¼ teaspoon cayenne (ground red pepper)

dash coarsely ground black peppercorns
vegetable oil
snipped fresh cilantro

Peel eggplant and cut into quarters. Cut each quarter into ½-inch-thick slices. In small bowl, combine salt, turmeric, cayenne, and black pepper. Sprinkle over both sides of eggplant. Add just enough oil to large skillet to coat bottom. Heat over medium heat. Add eggplant slices, a few at a time. Fry until golden brown on bottom. Turn and fry until other side is golden. Transfer to paper-towel-lined plate to drain. Fry remaining eggplant slices, adding oil to skillet as needed. Sprinkle with cilantro. Serve immediately. Makes 4 servings.

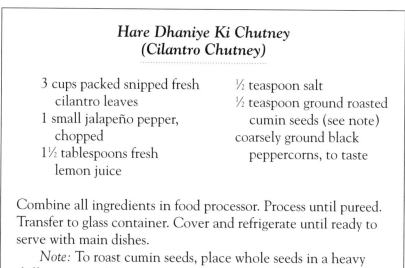

Hare Dhaniye Ki Chutney
(Cilantro Chutney)

3 cups packed snipped fresh cilantro leaves
1 small jalapeño pepper, chopped
1½ tablespoons fresh lemon juice

½ teaspoon salt
½ teaspoon ground roasted cumin seeds (see note)
coarsely ground black peppercorns, to taste

Combine all ingredients in food processor. Process until pureed. Transfer to glass container. Cover and refrigerate until ready to serve with main dishes.

Note: To roast cumin seeds, place whole seeds in a heavy skillet over medium heat. Stir constantly until darkened. Grind.

Vegetarian Samosas

4 cups all-purpose flour
½ teaspoon ground turmeric
½ teaspoon salt
½ cup ghee (see page 119)
1 cup milk
1 teaspoon fresh lemon juice

filling (below)
additional milk
vegetable oil
plain yogurt

In large bowl, combine flour, turmeric, and salt. Add ghee, pressing with back of spoon to combine. In separate bowl, combine milk and lemon juice. Stir into flour mixture. Continue stirring until soft dough forms. (Add small amount of additional milk or flour to dough as needed for soft but not sticky consistency.) Cover with damp cloth and set aside. Prepare filling. Roll out dough to about ¼ inch thickness on lightly floured surface. Cut out sixteen 5-inch rounds. Cut each round in half. Top each half with generous teaspoonful of filling. Brush edges of dough with milk. Fold dough over filling to form triangle. Seal and crimp edges with fork. In large, deep saucepan, heat about 2 inches of vegetable oil over medium heat until hot. Slide samosas into hot oil, a few at a time. Fry slowly until crisp and golden brown, turning frequently. Drain on paper-towel-lined plate. Serve warm or at room temperature with yogurt. Makes about 32.

Filling: Peel and boil 2 medium potatoes in water 20 minutes or until very tender. Drain and mash. Set aside. Drain 1 can (14 ounces) artichoke hearts. Puree in blender or food processor. Mix into mashed potatoes. In large skillet, heat 2 teaspoons coriander seeds, 1 teaspoon cumin seeds, and ½ teaspoon fenugreek seeds until lightly roasted, stirring constantly. Remove from heat and cool to room temperature. Grind and toss with 1 teaspoon coarsely ground black peppercorns. Stir into mashed potato mixture. Add 2 peeled and chopped tomatoes and ½ cup cooked peas.

Greece

A Way to Cook, the Way to Go

When the Turks conquered the Greeks centuries ago, the chefs that fled Greece carried their treasured recipes with them to protected Orthodox monasteries. These chefs, perpetuating their culinary traditions within the monastery walls, wore white hats to distinguish themselves from the priests, who wore black. The tall chefs' hats worn today originated from this ancient Greek practice.

The Greeks began their migration to Pennsylvania around the turn of the twentieth century, most arriving between 1900 and 1915. Many were solid entrepreneurs, opening dry cleaners, movie theaters, confectionery shops, and restaurants, where they exercised the cooking techniques they celebrated with such a passion.

Nowadays, Greek food is extremely popular in the United States, and recipes are often appropriate for or sometimes adapted to meet the "lighter" preferences of many health-conscious Americans. Olive oil, fresh garlic, and herbs such as oregano, especially a wild oregano called rigani, are used abundantly in the Greek kitchen, and baking or roasting meat is preferred to frying.

Meat means lamb to most Greeks, and it is used in a variety of main dishes. Whole lambs are stuffed and roasted for the Easter celebration, fricasseed, or cubed and cooked in soups and stews. Veal and beef are not as popular, and very little pork is used in Greek cuisine. The Greeks love chicken and fish, however, and use them often. Tomatoes and tomato paste are commonly seasoned with onions and garlic and cooked with meat to create some wonderful main dishes and sauces.

Greek side dishes may include one of several varieties of olives, such as Calamata (or Kalamata), a brine-cured and slit black olive packed in vinegar, or Nafplion, a brine-cured and cracked dark green olive packed in olive oil. Cheese is also served on the side, in main dishes, salads, and appetizers. Feta cheese, made with sheep's or goat's milk, is the best-known and most popular cheese among the Greeks and just about anyone who loves Greek cooking. Feta is used in salads or served with crackers or crisp bread. Kefaloteri, a hard cheese, is also popular and more often used in meat, pasta, and fresh vegetable dishes.

Greek phyllo (also spelled filo) is a paper-thin dough most commonly used in Greek pastries like baklava. Making the dough from scratch is labor intensive and requires at least two people, so you may want to consider using a high-quality, commercially made phyllo dough in recipes that call for it.

Ouzo (pronounced "oo-zoe"), an unsweetened anise-flavored liqueur, is the national drink of Greece and remains popular among Greek-Americans. Traditionally, ouzo is served with appetizers, or *mezethes*, such as cheese, olives, tomatoes, and lemon wedges. Retsina, a popular Greek wine, is produced only in Greece and is imported to the United States.

For Christmas in 1972, Mom and Dad gave me a small Greek cookbook, called *Can the Greeks Cook!* (The Dietz Press, 1969). I still love that book, even though the pages are yellowing and there are no four-color photographs of the food. Authors Fannie Venos and Lillian Prichard did a wonderful job of describing Greek tradition and presenting classic recipes that anyone can make.

The Simple Art of Greek Cooking (Perigee Books, 1990), by Anna and John Spanos, is another wonderful cookbook for people who want to cook in the traditional Greek style. The recipes are easy and use readily available ingredients.

Additionally, you can seek out most any Greek Orthodox church for authentic recipes, ingredient sources, and food festivals. I've selected three Pennsylvania-based Greek festivals to describe here, although there are many more. You can contact a church in your area for more information on local Greek-oriented activities.

In the middle of a heavy May rain, I struck out for the Oakland area of Pittsburgh to visit the St. Nicholas Greek Food Festival. I had learned from members of a Greek Orthodox church that this was probably the largest event of its kind in Pennsylvania.

Parishioner volunteers from the St. Nicholas Greek Orthodox Cathedral have held the mammoth event for more than thirty-five years now and have the Pittsburgh-area festival down to a science. Most of the fifty-some men, women, and children who prepare the food are descendants of many generations of Greek cooks and prepare the festival dishes in their homes, restaurants, and the cathedral itself.

The festival attracts close to 30,000 people annually and, as a result, requires huge quantities of food: 10,250 souzoukakia (meatballs in wine sauce), 265 huge pans of moussaka (baked eggplant), almost 2,000 pounds of lamb for souvlakia (shish kebab), and 2,800 pounds of marinated chicken. Cooks were also busy making 13,000 dolmathes, or stuffed grape leaves. And as difficult as it may have been, bakers made 10,500 servings of that delicious dessert called baklava.

Spanakopita, thin layers of flaky pastry filled with spinach and feta, was the most popular dish at the festival and was excellent. Children especially enjoyed the pastitsio, layers of macaroni, grated cheese, and ground beef baked in a rich cream sauce. Dinners included beef stefatho (beef cubes braised with onions in an aromatic sauce), chicken oregano (half a chicken marinated in olive oil, lemon, and oregano, then baked), fish plaki (seasoned haddock with tomatoes and onions), and souvlakia. The dinners came with a buttery rice pilaf.

A classic Greek salad, full of Greek olives and feta cheese and dressed with a delicate blend of olive oil, lemon juice, and vinegar, was also served. There were plenty of side dishes, too, like tiropeta, layers of phyllo filled and baked with several cheeses and eggs, and green beans simmered with zucchini in tomato sauce.

The desserts were abundant, several, including baklava, karithopeta (a rich walnut cake), galatoboureko (baked custard), and kataife (shredded pastry layered with nuts), served with a rich honey syrup. Light, fluffy puffs of golden pastry called loukoumades were also served with honey and seemed to be the most popular item on the dessert table. There also were Greek butter cookies and moist, oval cinnamon cookies called finikia. While we ate our dessert, vibrantly costumed parishioner children danced to Greek music.

Foods are priced à la carte, ranging from 50 cents for a dolmathe to $4.95 to $5.95 for dinner. Greek cookbooks are available for $4 and festival gift certificates for $10 each. Profits help the various causes supported by the St. Nicholas Greek Orthodox Cathedral.

The St. Nicholas Greek Food Festival is held during the first or second week in May for lunch and dinner. Call (412) 682-3866 for more information and specific hours of operation.

Spanakopita (Spinach Pie)

1 pound (2 cups) melted
  butter, divided
1 medium onion, finely chopped
2 pounds fresh spinach, washed,
  drained well, and torn
1 pound crumbled feta cheese

7 eggs, slightly beaten
salt and coarsely ground
  black pepper, to taste
½ pound phyllo pastry
  sheets

In large skillet, heat 1 tablespoon of the butter over medium high heat. Add onion. Sauté 3 minutes, or just until onion is tender. Remove from heat. Stir in spinach, feta cheese, and eggs. Salt and pepper to taste. Brush half of the phyllo sheets with melted butter and arrange, buttered side up, in bottom of lightly greased 13×9-inch baking pan. Spoon and evenly spread spinach mixture over pastry in pan. Brush remaining phyllo sheets with melted butter and arrange over spinach mixture. Brush top with melted butter. Using sharp knife, lightly score top to make individual serving-size squares. Bake at 350 degrees for 30 minutes. (If top begins to brown too much during baking, cover with foil.) Cut into squares. Serve hot. Makes 10 to 12 servings.

Tiropeta (Baked Cheese Pudding)

1½ dozen eggs
1 pound cottage cheese
1 pound feta cheese, crumbled
½ cup milk or light cream
2 tablespoons all-purpose flour

1 cup butter, melted
½ pound phyllo pastry
  sheets

In large bowl, beat eggs lightly. Stir in cottage cheese and feta cheese, blending well. In small bowl, combine milk or cream and flour. Blend into egg-cheese mixture. Brush 4 sheets of phyllo with melted butter and arrange, buttered side up, in bottom of lightly greased 15×10-inch baking pan. Pour cheese mixture over pastry in pan. Brush remaining phyllo sheets with melted butter and arrange over cheese mixture. Brush top with melted butter. Bake at 350 degrees for 1 hour. (If top begins to brown too much during baking, cover with foil.) Cool and cut into squares. Makes 10 to 12 servings.

Dolmathes (Stuffed Grape Leaves)

1 cup uncooked rice
2 cups cold water
1 teaspoon salt
3 large onions, finely chopped
2 cups water, divided
1 cup olive oil
2 tablespoons tomato paste
salt and coarsely ground
　　black pepper, to taste

2 tablespoons snipped
　　fresh parsley
⅓ cup fresh lemon juice,
　　divided
1 jar (about 15 ounces)
　　grape leaves

Soak rice in 2 cups cold water with salt for 30 minutes. Drain and set aside. In large skillet, bring onions and 1 cup of the additional water to a boil. Reduce heat and cook 15 minutes or until tender. Add olive oil and cook 5 more minutes. Stir in soaked rice and tomato paste. Salt and pepper to taste. Cook 5 minutes. Add parsley. Cook 3 minutes. Add half of the lemon juice and cook 5 more minutes. Rinse and drain grape leaves. Lay leaves flat with shiny sides down. Place 1 teaspoon of rice mixture near stem end of each leaf. Starting at stem end, gently roll up leaves, tucking in sides and allowing small amount of room for rice to expand. Arrange in layers in large saucepan. Top with remaining lemon juice and 1 cup water. Weight down with heavy plate. Cover and bring to simmer over medium high heat. Reduce heat and simmer 40 to 45 minutes or until rice is tender. (Add water to pan as needed.) Drain and discard any excess cooking liquid. Cover and refrigerate grape leaves at least 3 hours. Serve cold. Makes 4 to 6 servings.

A little later in May, there's another Greek festival just across the Susquehanna River from Harrisburg. Located in Wormleysburg, this festival isn't as large as the Oakdale event near Pittsburgh, but it is the largest of its kind in the capital region. The food is wonderful, and women of the Holy Trinity Greek Orthodox Cathedral cook and bake for weeks in preparation for their church's three-day festival.

The festival is held both indoors and outside under tents. Outdoors, savory aromas lure visitors to sample fun-type Greek foods like gyros (ground meat sandwiches) and souvlakia (lamb kebabs), alone or on pita bread. It was very hot the day we went, so my daughter, Kelly, and I escaped the heat to the cathedral's cool, cafeteria-style auditorium, which was filled with delicious Greek food.

Against a backdrop of Greek folk music and dancing, I was happy to sample many of the same items I had tasted at the Pittsburgh Greek festival. There also were some different foods on the menu this time. In addition to the expected, but not at all disappointing, moussaka and chicken, there was a wonderful lamb dinner served with a classic Greek salad, rice, and green beans for just $8. There were also generous portions of spanakopita, tiropeta, pastitsio, and dolmathes.

The church offered Greek-style meatballs, here called keftedes. (These are generally served at weddings, picnics, and most any Greek gathering or celebration.) Having failed in my own previous attempts to find a decent meatball recipe (or maybe it's just the cook), I was intrigued by Holy Trinity's meatballs, which were tender, moist, and perfectly seasoned. I decided to kitchen-test a Greek version. Armed with a battery of Greek cookbooks and a family of reluctant taste-testers, I devised my own Greek meatball recipe, as follows.

Baked Meatballs, Greek-Style

1 pound lean ground beef
  or lamb
1 cup canned vegetable broth
1 cup unseasoned, fine, dry
  bread crumbs
2 medium onions, finely chopped
2 tablespoons finely chopped
  fresh mint

1 teaspoon salt
⅛ teaspoon coarsely
  ground black pepper
1 can (28 ounces) crushed
  tomatoes
⅛ teaspoon cinnamon
hot cooked rice or pasta

In large bowl, thoroughly combine ground beef or lamb, vegetable broth, bread crumbs, onions, mint, salt, and pepper. Shape into 1½-inch balls. Layer in large casserole dish with crushed tomatoes. Sprinkle with cinnamon. Cover and bake at 400 degrees for 30 minutes. Remove cover and bake 30 more minutes. Serve over hot cooked rice or pasta. Makes 6 servings.

The festival also offered a sampler of fancy Greek pastries—including baklava, kataifi, loukoumades, karithopeta, and finikia—as well as koulourakia, rich egg Easter cookies, and kourambiethes, melt-in-your-mouth butter cookies. Greek coffee went especially well with these.

Moussaka, pastitsio, and other specialties served at the Holy Trinity Greek fest are available for takeout. There is ample free parking and no admission fee. The event is usually scheduled for Friday, Saturday, and Sunday in mid-May, and hours vary. For specifics, call (717) 763-7441.

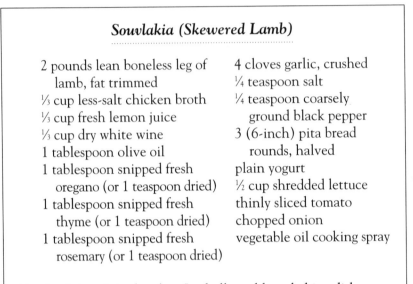

Souvlakia (Skewered Lamb)

2 pounds lean boneless leg of lamb, fat trimmed
⅓ cup less-salt chicken broth
⅓ cup fresh lemon juice
⅓ cup dry white wine
1 tablespoon olive oil
1 tablespoon snipped fresh oregano (or 1 teaspoon dried)
1 tablespoon snipped fresh thyme (or 1 teaspoon dried)
1 tablespoon snipped fresh rosemary (or 1 teaspoon dried)

4 cloves garlic, crushed
¼ teaspoon salt
¼ teaspoon coarsely ground black pepper
3 (6-inch) pita bread rounds, halved
plain yogurt
½ cup shredded lettuce
thinly sliced tomato
chopped onion
vegetable oil cooking spray

Cut lamb into 1-inch cubes. In shallow oblong baking dish, combine chicken broth, lemon juice, wine, olive oil, oregano, thyme, rosemary, garlic, salt, and pepper. Arrange lamb in mixture, turning to coat. Cover and refrigerate several hours or overnight. Thread lamb cubes on 6 skewers, reserving marinade. Lay skewers on broiler rack that has been lightly coated with cooking spray. Place rack over pan. Broil a few inches from heat for 10 minutes, occasionally turning and basting with reserved marinade. Stuff pita halves with lamb, yogurt, lettuce, tomato, and onions. Serve immediately. Makes 6 servings.

Moussaka (Baked Eggplant)

1 large (about 1½ pounds)
    eggplant
salt, to taste
about ⅓ cup olive oil, divided
1 pound ground lamb
1 large onion, finely chopped
½ cup dry red wine
¼ cup snipped fresh parsley
2 tablespoons tomato paste
1 clove garlic, crushed
1½ teaspoons salt, divided
¼ teaspoon dried oregano
¼ teaspoon cinnamon

⅛ teaspoon coarsely
    ground black pepper
⅛ teaspoon nutmeg
½ cup freshly grated
    Romano cheese, divided
2 eggs
1 egg yolk
2 tablespoons butter
2 tablespoons all-purpose
    flour
dash nutmeg
dash white pepper
2 cups milk

Remove stem end of eggplant. Cut in half lengthwise. (Do not peel.) Cut crosswise into ½-inch slices and sprinkle with salt. Arrange slices in single layer on clean paper towels. Top with additional paper towels, and weight down with heavy plate. Set aside 1 hour to drain. In large skillet, heat 1 tablespoon of the olive oil over medium high heat. Add lamb. Cook and stir until lightly browned. Drain off and discard excess liquid. Add onion to lamb. Sauté just until onions are tender. Stir in wine, parsley, tomato paste, garlic, 1 teaspoon of the salt, oregano, cinnamon, black pepper, and ⅛ teaspoon nutmeg. Bring to boil. Reduce heat. Cover and simmer 15 minutes. Remove cover and continue simmering 5 minutes, or until sauce thickens, stirring occasionally. Set aside. Pat dry eggplant with clean paper towels. Arrange in single layer in large, shallow baking pan. Brush with some of the remaining olive oil. Broil about 4 inches from heat for 5 minutes, or until lightly browned on one side. Turn and brush other side with olive oil. Broil 5 minutes more, or just until lightly browned. Arrange half of the eggplant in 2-quart casserole dish. Top with lamb mixture. Sprinkle with 2 tablespoons Romano cheese. Cover with remaining eggplant. Sprinkle with 2 more tablespoons Romano cheese. Set aside. In small bowl, beat together eggs and egg yolk with fork. Set aside. In medium

Continued on next page

Moussaka—Continued from previous page

saucepan, melt butter over medium heat. Whisk in flour, remaining ½ teaspoon salt, dash nutmeg, and dash white pepper, blending well. Remove from heat. Gradually add milk, whisking constantly. Return to medium heat. Cook, whisking constantly, until thickened. Reduce heat to low. Whisk about ½ cup of the hot mixture into the beaten eggs, blending well. Return to mixture in saucepan. Cook and whisk over low heat 1 minute. Pour over eggplant mixture in casserole dish. Sprinkle with remaining Romano cheese. Bake at 350 degrees for 45 minutes to 1 hour, or until top is lightly browned. Cut into squares and serve hot. Makes 6 to 8 servings.

Each fall, the Saints Constantine and Helen Greek Orthodox Church in Reading holds a Greek Food Bazaar. The first floor of the church serves as a Greek Taverna. Although somewhat less romantic than dining in a real taverna (but what *could* be as romantic?), the bazaar did offer classic Greek entrées against a background of live Greek music and intricate dancing. Friday's menu included kalamari, or squid, served on a bed of rice pilaf. Saturday's special was moussaka, and Sunday's offering was a generous serving of roasted lamb on pilaf. Each entrée came with green beans, salad, roll, and butter for just $6. Large and small Greek salads brimming with Greek cheeses and olives were also available.

Spanakopita, tiropeta, keftedes, pastitsio, and dolmathes were also on the menu, as was a sampler that included taramosalata, a spread made with roe or caviar. There was also a delicious Greek rice pudding, different from the desserts I had sampled at the other festivals. There was an entire room devoted to pastry, and the homemade, honey-sweetened treats went well with the thick, strong Greek coffee. (To make Greek coffee, finely ground beans are brought to a boil in hot water to create an unusual foam. You then drink the coffee, grounds and all.)

The Saints Constantine and Helen Greek Orthodox Church holds its Greek Food Bazaar each October. In addition to sampling the delicious food, you can take a guided tour of the church, view Greek silk screening, and visit the gift shop. For more information, call (610) 374-7511 or write in care of the church, 1001 E. Wyomissing Blvd., Reading, PA 19611.

Taramosalata (Fish Roe Spread)

4 slices white bread, crusts
   removed
4 ounces red fish roe (tarama)
1 tablespoon grated onion

½ cup olive oil
juice of 1 lemon
snipped fresh parsley
assorted crackers

Lightly toast bread slices. Soak in water until saturated. Squeeze
dry. Place roe in food processor or blender. Cover and process
on lowest speed just until creamy. Add bread and onion, blending
on lowest speed. Gradually add olive oil and lemon juice,
blending on high speed until light in color and creamy. Garnish
with parsley and serve with assorted crackers. Makes 8 to
10 appetizer servings.

Salata me Feta ke Elies
(Greek Salad with Feta and Olives)

8 cups washed and torn
  romaine lettuce
4 cups washed and torn arugula
1 medium green bell pepper,
  julienned
1 medium red bell pepper,
  julienned
½ red onion, thinly sliced and
  separated into rings
½ cup drained, pitted
  Calamata olives
½ cup sliced radishes
2 large tomatoes, cut into
  thin wedges

¼ cup dry white wine
¼ cup fresh lemon juice
1 tablespoon olive oil
1 tablespoon snipped fresh
  oregano (or 1 teaspoon
  dried)
4 cloves garlic, crushed
¼ teaspoon salt
¼ teaspoon coarsely
  ground black pepper
½ cup crumbled feta
  cheese

In large serving bowl, toss lettuce, arugula, bell peppers, olives,
onion, radishes, and tomatoes. Set aside. In jar with tight-fitting
lid, combine wine, lemon juice, olive oil, oregano, garlic, salt,
and pepper. Cover tightly and shake well. Pour over salad, gently
tossing to coat. (If dressing is not used right away, shake again
just before serving.) Top with feta cheese and serve immediately.
Makes 8 to 10 servings.

It wasn't easy to get an interview with Pete Mantango. He was busy
making mints the day I called to ask some questions about his family
owned and operated Greek candy company. Two days later, I finally got
my interview. That's when I found out that Pete himself did most of the
hands-on work required to maintain his confectionery business, leaving
precious little time to talk with pesky food writers.

Pete said that he couldn't explain the Greek-American preoccupa-
tion with restaurant and candy enterprises. He was, however, happy to
talk in some detail about his family. Pete and his wife, Katherine, co-own
the business, and his mom, although semiretired, stays involved in the
day-to-day operations.

Pete's mom and dad were born in Tripoli, Greece, and came to
Pennsylvania some fifty years ago. His grandfather founded Mantangos

a few years after making candy for the now-defunct Pomeroy's Department Store. Decades later, Mantangos Candies still handcrafts and sells an assortment of yummy caramels, nougats, and buttercreams at about $8.50 to $10.95 a pound. Ivory-coated candies are a specialty there, and Pete says his grandfather invented this white chocolate coating so in demand everywhere today. The factory uses about 20,000 pounds of raw chocolate annually, which translates into almost 40,000 pounds of Greek-inspired confections.

Mantangos is located at 1501 Catherine St., between Derry and Paxton Streets in Harrisburg. The company also has an outlet at the Harrisburg East Mall and in addition to candy, sells terrific coffee drinks and pastries. For hours of operation and more information on both locations, call (717) 234-0882.

Not only does Harrisburg lay claim to Mantangos, but it's also home for the Greek owned and operated Gazebo Room Restaurant. The Gekas family cooks up some wonderful Greek- and American-style dishes in a comfy, cozy atmosphere on the corner of Second and Locust Streets, but the real prize may be the Gazebo Room's Greek salad dressing.

Family "chefs" originally dressed cold-cut subs with the classic Greek olive oil vinaigrette in a sandwich shop formerly around the corner. Since the early seventies, however, the Gazebo Room Restaurant has laid claim to this perfectly balanced salad accompaniment as its own house dressing. The product has withstood the taste test of more than two decades, and most customers prefer it to the typical French, Italian, or blue cheese.

"Patrons liked the dressing so much that they started bringing in their own containers and asking us to fill them with our Greek dressing so they could take some home," says Nick Gekas, co-owner (with brother, Steve) of the Mechanicsburg-based Gazebo Room Salad Dressing business. "Eventually we started gathering our own bottles, cleaning and filling them with dressing to sell in the restaurant." The business has grown to 15,000 cases distributed monthly in grocery stores throughout southeastern Pennsylvania, and the Gekas brothers don't have to gather empty bottles anymore. You can pick up a bottle for about $2.50 in many chain stores, including Fox's Market, Giant Foods, Weis Markets, Karns, or Festival Foods.

THE GREEK WEDDING

The traditional wedding ceremony of the Greek Orthodox Church begins with a greeting from the priest to the couple to be married. The couple walk arm in arm as they kiss the various icons placed along the altar, blessing themselves after each. The first part of the hour-long ceremony symbolizes the engagement. The priest places the ring on the right hand of the bride and then on the right hand of the groom. The rings are then interchanged three times to symbolize the Father, Son, and Holy Ghost. The koumbaro (best man) and koumbara (matron of honor) also exercise the ring exchange and become the godparents of the first child born to the couple.

At some point in the ceremony, the bride gently steps on the foot of her new husband to let him know that she intends to keep him under foot during the marriage. The priest then places orange blossom wreaths joined by a white satin ribbon on the heads of the bride and groom, and these are interchanged three times to symbolize the trinity.

The couple is showered with rice and Jordan almonds as they move around a large table in the center of the church. This is done to wish the couple a sweet life. Each guest receives a koofeta, or handful of Jordan almonds, for good luck. Young Greek girls sleep on the token so they will dream about the man they will marry.

To end the ceremony, wine is passed to the members of the wedding party. After the koumbaro takes a sip, he is slapped on the back of the neck for good luck, and if unmarried, it is said that he will marry next. Lavish receptions with lots of music, dancing, and food follow the ceremony.

During the ceremony, a family member or close friend remains at the couple's house to welcome them home afterward. The Greeks consider it bad luck for newlyweds to return to an empty house. Sometimes the couple break a rod across the doorway to symbolize their entrance to a new way of life.

Kourambiethes
(Wedding Cakes)

1 cup butter
½ cup confectioner's sugar
1 teaspoon vanilla extract
2¼ cups all-purpose flour

1 teaspoon salt
1 cup chopped almonds
additional confectioner's
  sugar

In large bowl, beat butter until softened. Add confectioner's sugar and vanilla extract, creaming well. Gradually blend in flour and salt. Stir in almonds. Roll dough into ¾-inch balls, and place on lightly greased baking sheets. Bake at 400 degrees for 12 to 14 minutes, or until very lightly browned. While warm, roll in additional confectioner's sugar. Cool completely on wire racks. Makes about 2 dozen.

Africa

Foods of Kwanzaa and More

Unlike other immigrants, African-Americans came to the colonies against their will, as slaves. Most claimed West Africa as their real home.

Philadelphia served as a major port of arrival for slaves, and in the 1730s, slavery for the purpose of skilled labor increased throughout the state. Unlike the plantation economy of the South, Pennsylvania's slaves generally worked alongside their masters as bakers, carpenters, domestic servants, and such.

Increasing demands for slave labor also brought more protests among Pennsylvanians, especially Quakers, to abolish the practice. This led to a ban on slave importation in Pennsylvania in 1767. In 1780, Pennsylvania formally began the process of ending slavery with an emancipation law that stated that no African-American born after 1780 within the state would be enslaved past the age of twenty-eight. With this law, Pennsylvania became the first state to outlaw slavery, at least to some extent.

Pennsylvania's growing African-American community was centered in Philadelphia, and it was there that support groups such as the Free African Society and the Society for the Relief of Free Negroes were formed. These groups fought for the rights and freedom of black Americans and helped abolish slavery altogether through the end of the Civil War.

When the Civil War ended, many freed African-Americans from the southern states migrated to Pennsylvania seeking better jobs and wages. Many found work in the steel industry around Pittsburgh and Steelton, the coal mines of southwestern Pennsylvania, the railroads in Erie and Harrisburg, and Philadelphia's shipyards. Others became entrepreneurs—caterers, insurers, barbers, beauticians, and the like. Although their lives were improving, the majority still struggled with prejudice and poor living conditions.

Today, African-Americans constitute the fifth-largest ethnic group in Pennsylvania, and as a result, their culture and customs have had significant impact on the state. A growing number of African-American events are held throughout the year in many parts of the commonwealth as one way to increase cultural awareness and understanding about the African-American community.

Most African countries are agricultural in nature. The men work as farmers, cattle ranchers, or fishermen, and in some regions, the women are responsible for planting and harvesting the crops. Women also prepare the meals, turning the harvest into simple dishes such as fufu—pounded yams roasted over open pits and served with soups, meats, and a variety of sauces.

Several different tribal nations made up the slave population in the American South, and as a result, regional African recipes were freely exchanged and integrated with other styles of cooking. Native Americans taught black Americans how to cook with local plants, and these methods contributed to a multinational cuisine among African-Americans.

During colonial times, heavy breakfasts of cornmeal cakes, called hoecakes, and molasses fueled the slaves for long days of intense physical labor. Other corn dishes such as spoonbread, corn pone, corn pudding, and succotash were integral to the African-American diet, providing sound nutrition for hard work. Crab cakes and various leafy green vegetables were common, too.

During the Civil War, African-Americans cooked for both the Northern and Southern armies and, as a result of shortages, were forced to improvise dishes and create original recipes from the meager ingredients they had on hand. Creole and Cajun cooking techniques originated with the War Between the States, and dishes like jambalaya, dirty rice, and gumbo remain trendy in restaurants and homes all over the country.

"Soul food" evolved from African-American eateries of the early 1900s. These restaurants specialized in southern fried chicken, fish, pork chops, potato salad, and rice and gravy. Later on, pigs' feet, chitlins (or chitterlings—hog intestines), collard greens, and ham were added to the soul food menu and are still popular at many African-American celebrations today.

Blair County's African American Heritage Project offers a wide assortment of soul food at its annual midsummer festival. Along with African-American music, dancing, lectures, and crafts, you'll find lots of crisp, southern fried chicken, cooked and perfectly seasoned collards, fresh potato salad, and scrumptious sweet potato pie. Festival coordinator William Lightner swears that Ribbin's, a vendor shipped in from Chambersburg, offers the best barbecued pork and beef ribs in the world. "They melt in your mouth," says Will.

Caribbean foods are also in demand at the Blair County fest. There's curried rice and jerk chicken, a tangy dish for those who enjoy spicy seasoning on their poultry. The grilled barbecued goat may be unusual for Altoona but is ready for sampling at the festival. Fish, hot dogs, burgers, and sausage are available for the less adventuresome. Most platters, exotic or otherwise, run about $5.

The African American Heritage Project of Blair County is held one Saturday, usually in July, from 10 A.M. until 8 P.M. at the Penn State Altoona Campus. There are no fees for admission or parking. For more information, contact the Railroader's Memorial Museum, 1300 Ninth Ave., Altoona, PA 16602, telephone (814) 946-0834.

Barbecued Pork Ribs

about 6 pounds country-style pork ribs or back ribs, cut in slabs
salt and coarsely ground black pepper, to taste
1½ cups water
1 can (6 ounces) tomato paste
2 tablespoons dark molasses
1 tablespoon sugar
1 tablespoon packed brown sugar
1 teaspoon Worcestershire sauce
1 teaspoon brown mustard
½ teaspoon salt
½ teaspoon garlic powder
¼ teaspoon hot pepper sauce

Arrange ribs in large baking dish or roasting pan. Salt and pepper to taste. Cover loosely with foil. Bake at 350 degrees for 30 minutes. Turn and bake an additional 30 minutes. Drain excess liquid. Meanwhile, in medium saucepan, combine water, tomato paste, molasses, sugar, brown sugar, Worcestershire sauce, mustard, salt, garlic powder, and hot pepper sauce. Bring to soft boil over medium high heat. Reduce heat and simmer 15 minutes. Pour sauce over partially baked ribs, turning to coat. Bake additional 1 hour or until browned and very tender, turning once and basting occasionally during baking. Makes 6 to 8 servings.

You can also enjoy a Soul Food Sampling at Pittsburgh's North Area YWCA every February in honor of Black History Month. Parents of YWCA youths make fried chicken, corn bread, greens (collard, mustard, and turnip), black-eyed peas, macaroni and cheese, and sweet potato pie. Generous servings run $5 per adult and $3 per child, and you won't go away hungry.

The YWCA's Soul Food Sampling is held the third to last Sunday in February. Kids ages seven to seventeen perform and make crafts at the event, too. Proceeds benefit the YWCA. The North Area YWCA is located just outside Pittsburgh at 8500 Thompson Run Rd., Alison Park, PA 15101. For more information, call (412) 366-4381.

Southern Fried Chicken

2 large chicken fryers, cut up
salt, to taste
1 cup milk
1 egg
2 cups all-purpose flour
2 tablespoons paprika
2 teaspoons salt
1 teaspoon white pepper
dash cayenne (ground
  red pepper)
about 5 cups solid
  vegetable shortening

Pat chicken dry with paper towels and sprinkle with salt. Cover and refrigerate several hours or overnight. About 2 hours before serving, in small bowl, combine milk and egg. In separate shallow bowl, combine flour, paprika, salt, white pepper, and cayenne. Dip chicken pieces in milk mixture. Dredge through flour mixture, coating well. Shake off excess coating. Let stand 30 minutes. In deep-fat fryer or kettle, melt shortening and heat to 365 degrees. Fry chicken, a few pieces at a time, in hot fat 15 minutes per side, or until golden brown. Remove from fat with tongs and drain on paper-towel-lined tray. Serve hot. Makes 6 to 8 servings.

Country Collard Greens

2 bunches fresh collard greens
1 tablespoon lard
1 medium onion, finely
chopped
½ pound thick-sliced bacon,
cut up

2 cups water
salt and coarsely ground
black pepper, to taste
1 to 2 drops hot pepper
sauce

Trim and discard coarse stems from collard greens. Place leaves and tender stems in large bowl. Cover with lukewarm water. Let stand 5 minutes. Drain. Rinse and drain a few times. In large saucepan, melt lard over medium high heat. Add onions and bacon, and sauté 5 minutes, or until bacon begins to brown. Add collard greens and water. Bring to boil. Reduce heat and cover. Cook 20 minutes, or until greens are crisp-tender. Remove cover. Increase heat to high, and boil until most of the water evaporates. Salt and pepper to taste. Add hot sauce. Makes 6 servings.

Buttermilk Corn Muffins

1 cup yellow cornmeal
1 cup all-purpose flour
¼ cup sugar
2 teaspoons baking powder
½ teaspoon baking soda

½ teaspoon salt
1 cup buttermilk
2 tablespoons vegetable oil
1 egg

In large bowl, combine cornmeal, flour, sugar, baking powder, baking soda, and salt. In separate bowl, beat buttermilk, oil, and egg with fork. Add all at once to cornmeal mixture. Mix with spoon just until dry ingredients are moistened. Fill lightly greased muffin tins or corn stick pans about ¾ full with batter. Bake at 425 degrees for 15 to 18 minutes, or until golden brown. Serve warm. Makes about 1 dozen.

Clinton Haughton makes a "mean" curried chicken. With Jamaican roots and formal training in classic French cooking, Clinton has very successfully blended a variety of culinary techniques with African-American methods to create wonderful, somewhat unusual menus for his Maryland-based business, Exotic Tropic Caterers. I caught up with him at the African Family Festival in Harrisburg's Reservoir Park.

Clinton's menu board listed jerk chicken at the top. His version was a spicy combination of chicken with scallions, pimentos, cloves, black pepper, salt, and a multicolored, oblong hot pepper called Scotch bonnet. I liked the curried chicken and goat dishes, too. (The goat comes from a Washington, D.C., supplier.) The braised oxtail was modestly seasoned with onions, salt, and pepper and served in a velvety brown sauce over rice and beans.

There were some great creole dishes on Clinton's menu. The creole fish dinner consisted of breaded, not-too-spicy fried fish served over rice and beans with a side of roasted bell peppers, carrots, and cabbage. (I've had similar dishes in fine restaurants, and this one was a strong competitor.) This fish made a great sandwich, too. Another fish dish was escoveitch, a pan-fried whole fish, usually red snapper, served with a sprinkling of hot pepper vinaigrette. It's very common in the Caribbean, and the vinaigrette makes it.

Prices were very reasonable at the Exotic Tropic Caterers tent. If you're interested in a catered event, call (301) 773-2158.

There were plenty of other food and craft vendors at Harrisburg's African Family Festival. A New York–based caterer called Nyota's Ting offered an extensive menu with foods appropriate for dieters, vegetarians, and anyone who enjoys whole foods. The display of Ting's dishes looked very appetizing and included pineapple chicken, curried chick peas with vegetables, tofu salad, and vegetable lasagna. Judging by the crowd around this particular booth, the food was very popular.

The average price for a complete dinner at the Nyota's Ting booth was about $7. Call (718) 217-0583 for more information on available catering services.

Harrisburg's African Family Festival also features soul food, an African marketplace, live entertainment, and cultural information. Ngozi, Inc., a nonprofit educational organization, sponsors the festival, and about 8,000 people attend each year. The event is held on a Sunday in mid-June from 11 A.M. until dusk. Admission is free, and parking costs $1. For more information, call (717) 234-7724.

Jerk Chicken

2 tablespoons whole allspice

4 green onions, minced

2 cloves garlic, minced

1 hot green or red chili pepper, seeded and minced

2 tablespoons fresh lime juice

1 tablespoon snipped fresh thyme

½ teaspoon salt

¼ teaspoon freshly grated nutmeg

¼ cup olive oil

6 boneless, skinless chicken breast halves

Using a mortar and pestle or food grinder, crush allspice until fine. In large shallow bowl, toss crushed allspice with green onions, garlic, chili pepper, lime juice, thyme, salt, and nutmeg. Gradually add olive oil, blending until paste forms. Pat chicken dry with paper towels. Dredge through spice mixture, turning to coat. Transfer to large dish. Cover and refrigerate several hours or overnight. Arrange on grill a few inches from medium hot coals. Cover and grill 10 minutes per side, or until tender and juices run clear. Serve immediately. Makes 6 servings.

Dirty Rice

4 thick slices bacon, cut into
pieces
1 medium onion, chopped
1 green bell pepper, diced
1 stalk celery, chopped
1 clove garlic, minced
2 tablespoons all-purpose flour
1 pound chicken livers
2½ cups water
½ teaspoon salt

½ teaspoon poultry
seasoning
¼ teaspoon dried thyme
¼ teaspoon coarsely
ground black pepper
⅛ teaspoon cayenne
(ground red pepper)
1¼ cups long-grain white
rice, uncooked

In large saucepan, cook bacon over medium heat 5 minutes, or
until browned and crisp, stirring frequently. Remove bacon from
pan and drain on paper towels. To bacon grease in saucepan, add
onion, bell pepper, celery, and garlic. Sauté 5 minutes. Add
flour, stirring 1 minute. Remove from heat. In food processor,
puree chicken livers. Add to onion mixture in saucepan. Return
to medium heat. Cook and stir 3 minutes, or until liver browns
and becomes almost solid. Stir in water, salt, poultry seasoning,
thyme, black pepper, and cayenne. Bring to boil, stirring
frequently. Add rice and return to boil. Reduce heat. Cover and
cook 20 minutes, or until rice is tender and liquid is absorbed.
Serve hot. Makes 6 to 8 servings.

Hoppin' John

1 pound dry black-eyed peas,
  rinsed and drained
1 pound ground sausage
1 medium onion, finely chopped
2 cloves garlic, minced
2 quarts water
2 tablespoons crushed hot red
  pepper flakes

1½ teaspoons white pepper
4 cups beef broth
2 tablespoons sweet
  (unsalted) butter
1 teaspoon salt
3 cups long-grain white
  rice, uncooked

In large bowl, cover peas with cold water. Cover and soak overnight in refrigerator. Drain. In Dutch oven or large kettle, cook sausage, onion and garlic over medium heat 10 minutes, or until sausage is lightly browned, stirring constantly. Drain excess liquid. Add soaked and drained peas, water, hot pepper flakes, and white pepper. Bring to boil. Reduce heat. Cover and simmer at least 1 hour or until peas are tender. Meanwhile, in separate saucepan, bring beef broth, butter, and salt to boil. Stir in rice. Reduce heat. Cover and cook 20 minutes, or until rice is tender and liquid absorbed. Spoon into large serving bowl. Top with black-eyed peas. Serve immediately. Makes 8 servings.

KWANZAA

Kwanzaa, a Swahili word meaning "first fruits of the harvest," is a relatively new celebration of family, culture, and ancestry observed by some 5 million African-Americans between December 26 and January 1 of each year. In 1966, Dr. Maulana Karenga initiated the holiday to promote unity and pride among people of African descent. Dr. Karenga's concept evolved from the tradition of Africa's agricultural people, who routinely gave thanks for their bountiful harvests.

The Kwanzaa Karamu, a lavish feast with music, dancing, and friendly discussion, is prepared on December 31. There is no one traditional food appropriate for Karamu, and the meal is often customized with dishes from Africa, the Caribbean, and South America. For some wonderful recipe ideas and a detailed explanation of Kwanzaa, read *Kwanzaa: An African American Celebration of Culture and Cooking*, by Eric V. Copage (William Morrow and Company, 1991).

Kwanzaa celebrations can be intimate and family-oriented or huge, pulling together African-Americans from all parts of a community. At Harrisburg Area Community College (HACC), some 200 people descend upon the International Room at the Cooper Student Center for a Friday evening Kwanzaa reception. There's plenty of entertainment—dramatic skits about diversity, hands-on multimedia activities for children, and African exhibits such as masks and musical instruments. The reception also includes an ethnic buffet prepared by a local African-American vendor, Pierce Catering. You can enjoy savory black-eyed peas and rice, corn bread, sweet potato tarts, and a delicious fruit punch.

The Saturday following the reception marks the main Kwanzaa celebration at HACC. Close to 1,000 people enjoy a full day of African entertainment, including jazz musicians, a precision drill team, gospel music, and a fashion show, as well as free health screenings. In the children's room, kids can make unique crafts and get a nutritious snack, while Mom and Dad browse the African craft and food kiosks.

Clinton Haughton, whom I met at Harrisburg's African Family Festival, also supplies HACC's festival with his wonderful creole fish and barbecue chicken. Local churches and area families are also there selling fried chicken, potato salad, greens, and sweet potato pie. If you're still hungry, there's even an African-American vendor, Angela's Festival Foods, selling funnel cakes and kielbasa—sort of a German-African-American culinary perspective. And for less exotic palates, there are also good ol' hot dogs, sodas, and classic baked goods.

HACC's Kwanzaa celebrations are held the first weekend in December at the school's Cooper Student Center. There is no admission fee for Friday or Saturday events, and the ample parking is free as well. For more information, call (717) 780-2632.

Shippensburg University holds its own Kwanzaa celebration in December. Hundreds of people eager to celebrate their African-American heritage and learn more about other cultures, too, enjoy a week of multicultural activities topped off by a Saturday buffet of Islamic and Caribbean foods, as well as those native to Africa.

Community volunteers work with Shippensburg University's food service department to prepare the Kwanzaa buffet. The menu includes spicy Caribbean beans and rice and an unusual Islamic white bean pie sweetened with brown sugar and sliced for dessert. Sweet potato pie is served, too, as well as a Kwanzaa fruit salad, consisting of apples, bananas, grapes, and nuts, to represent the "fruits of labor." Like so many holiday dinners, this one includes baked chicken and candied sweet potatoes, and the macaroni and cheese draws a crowd of children every time.

Shippensburg University holds its Kwanzaa festival during the first or second week of December at the Cumberland Union Building (CUB). This free event is sponsored by the campus African American Organization in cooperation with the school's Multi-Cultural Student Affairs Department. For more information, call (717) 532-1616.

White Bean Stew

4 cups drained canned white beans, liquid reserved
2 tablespoons vegetable oil
2 cups sliced carrots
1 cup chopped onion
3 leeks, sliced
1 clove garlic, minced
2 cups peeled and cubed sweet potatoes or yams
2 cups peeled and cubed turnips

1 cup peeled and cubed kohlrabi
½ cup snipped fresh parsley
2 bay leaves
1 teaspoon dried thyme
3 whole cloves
2 cups packed washed and torn fresh spinach
1 to 2 teaspoons soy sauce

Pour reserved bean liquid into 4-cup measure. Add enough water to make 4 cups total liquid and set aside. In Dutch oven or large kettle, heat oil over medium high heat. Add carrots, onion, leeks, and garlic. Sauté 5 minutes. Add beans, reserved 4 cups liquid, sweet potatoes or yams, turnips, kohlrabi, parsley, bay leaves, thyme and cloves. Cover and cook 1 hour, or until vegetables are tender. Adjust liquid as needed for desired consistency. Add spinach and soy sauce. Cover and simmer additional 20 minutes. Remove and discard bay leaves and whole cloves. Serve hot. Makes 6 servings.

Sweet Potato–Walnut Pie

4 medium sweet potatoes
  with skins
⅔ cup honey
½ teaspoon ground cinnamon
½ teaspoon ground ginger
½ teaspoon ground nutmeg
3 eggs
1½ cups light cream

9-inch unbaked pastry crust
3 tablespoons sweet
  (unsalted) butter
3 tablespoons honey
½ cup coarsely chopped
  walnuts
sweetened whipped cream
  (optional)

Preheat oven to 425 degrees. In large saucepan, cover sweet potatoes with water. Cover pan and bring to boil. Reduce heat and cook 25 minutes, or until very tender. Drain and cool slightly. Remove skins and mash potatoes until smooth. Place in food processor with ⅔ cup honey, cinnamon, ginger, nutmeg, eggs, and cream. Process just until blended and smooth. Pour into unbaked crust. Place in preheated oven. Immediately reduce oven temperature to 350 degrees. Bake 50 minutes, or until almost set. Remove from oven and cool to room temperature on wire rack. In small saucepan, melt butter. Add 3 tablespoons honey. Bring to boil, stirring constantly. Remove from heat. Stir in walnuts. Spoon evenly over cooled pie. Let stand until topping is cooled. Serve with sweetened whipped cream, if desired. Makes 6 to 8 servings.

Middle East

Jewish Foods, Tradition, and Travel

The Jewish religion is one of the oldest, dating back to about 1700 B.C. with the patriarch Abraham. Jews thrived in ancient Roman and Persian empires but, unhappy with their station in life, rebelled and lost their homeland in the second century A.D. Two basic groups of Jewish people emerged during the Middle Ages: the Mediterranean Jews of Arab lands, called Sephardic, and those of Christian Europe, known as Ashkenazic.

Although the Middle Ages proved difficult for Jews as a result of prejudice and persecution, more liberal attitudes during the eighteenth and nineteenth centuries allowed Jewish people full rights of citizenship, at least for those who lived in western Europe and Germany. However, the Jewish Reform movement in Germany left many Jews with a dilemma: either "blend in" by giving up their traditional dress, diet, and customs, or go elsewhere. In Russia, Orthodox Jews experienced even greater oppression, and as a result, many left for the American colonies.

Jews first settled in the commonwealth in the 1730s. Most headed for Philadelphia, Pittsburgh, and Easton, but a handful of families made homes in Lancaster and Schaefferstown, as well.

Although many immigrants relied on their agricultural skills and Pennsylvania's rich earth to make a living, not so with the Jewish people, most of whom came as peddlers and merchants—a few at first, and then more to major cities where they could set up shop and draw large numbers of customers. Some Jews were even licensed to trade with the Native Americans.

Today, Philadelphia has the fourth-largest population of Jews among U.S. cities, and Jewish communities flourish throughout the commonwealth. Immigrant Jews passed down their traditions within the home, but today religious schools are often the source of information about Jewish tradition, and children learn Hebrew and essential customs early on.

Jewish traditions generally derive from the practice of Judaism, and the most important beliefs stem from the mitzvoth, 613 holy obligations in the Torah and Talmud. These obligations include both positive and negative commandments ("Thou shall . . ." and "Thou shall not . . ."), and in modern times, Jews are expected to observe only a realistic number of these.

Jewish cuisine is closely tied to religious beliefs, which specify lists of permissible and impermissible foods. Orthodox Jews observe kashrut, a system of food laws for eating kosher foods and avoiding trefa foods.

161

Kosher foods are items specified as fit for consumption according to religious decree and include fruits, vegetables, grains, fish with scales and fins, domesticated birds, milk and eggs from kosher mammals and birds, and meat from cud-chewing mammals with split hooves. Trefa foods include meat from unkosher animals (pigs, rabbits, horses), birds of prey, such as owls and eagles; and water animals that do not have scales and fins, such as lobsters and crabs.

Kashrut also specifies that the slaughter of animals be painless. As a result, the Jewish butcher (shohet) studies animal anatomy to determine the precise spot on an animal's body for a quick and pain-free death. After the animal is killed, it must be drained of all blood and diseased portions eliminated. According to kashrut, meat and milk must be kept separate, and as a result, meat and dairy products are not prepared or eaten together by practicing Jews.

It's impossible to separate food from Jewish religious celebrations, and who would want to? The food customs have such colorful historical and religious significance.

SUKKOT

Sukkot is one of three major festivals on the Jewish lunar calendar (Passover and Shavuot are the other two). It falls two weeks after Rosh Hashanah. Sukkot commemorates the journey of the children of Israel through the desert after the exodus from Egypt. Unable to build permanent housing, the Israelites lived in temporary booths called *sukkots*.

During the modern-day Sukkot, Jews are supposed to eat and spend at least some leisure time in a makeshift sukkot "booth," and guests are often invited to share a meal within the walls of this customary dwelling. There are many rituals tied to celebrations within the sukkot, most focusing on nature and agriculture.

Sukkot Coffeecake

1 cup regular stick margarine
1 cup sugar
3 eggs
1 teaspoon vanilla extract
2½ cups unbleached
　　all-purpose flour
2 teaspoons baking powder

1 teaspoon baking soda
1 cup plain yogurt
3 tart apples, peeled and
　　sliced
walnut topping (below)
vegetable oil cooking spray

In large bowl, beat margarine until softened. Add sugar. Cream until light and fluffy. Add eggs one at a time, beating well after each addition. Blend in vanilla extract. In separate bowl, combine flour, baking powder, and baking soda. Add alternately with yogurt to creamed mixture. Spoon and evenly spread half of batter into 9-inch tube pan that has been lightly coated with cooking spray. Arrange half of the apple slices over batter in pan. Sprinkle with half of the walnut topping. Spoon and spread remaining batter over top. Top with remaining apples and topping. Bake at 375 degrees for 45 minutes. Cool in pan about 15 minutes. Remove from pan and cool completely. Makes 8 to 10 servings.

Walnut Topping: In small bowl, combine 1 cup chopped walnuts, ¼ cup sugar, and 2 teaspoons cinnamon, tossing to blend.

PASSOVER

Like Sukkot, Passover commemorates the exodus from Egypt and the freedom of the Jewish people from bondage, a time to give thanks for people all over the world who have been freed recently from suffering and oppression. It also marks the passage from the cold winter to warmer spring.

The Passover seder, the Hebrew word for order, helps re-create the Jews' flight from Egypt, and specific foods are eaten to symbolize the departure. Each of the foods is placed on a special seder plate in ceremonial order and with specific meaning and purpose. Karpas, or greens, are dipped in salt water to symbolize the coming of spring and the tears of the ancient Israelites while in bondage. Parsley is often used for the karpas. Lettuce, horseradish, or endive is also placed on the seder plate to symbolize a bitter herb, or maror, eaten in remembrance of the suffering of Egyptian slaves. Charoset, a mixture of apples, nuts, cinnamon, ginger, and wine, is eaten on unleavened bread, or matzoh, to resemble the bricks and mortar used by the children of Israel to build Egyptian cities for the pharoah Ramses. Three additional pieces of matzoh, "the bread of affliction," are served on a separate, covered plate as a reminder of the Jews' quick flight from Egypt with no time to wait for their bread to rise. The shank bone of a lamb, called tzroa, is placed on the seder plate to symbolize the original Passover ceremony known as Pesach, and finally, a roasted egg, called the baytza, is placed on the plate to symbolize rebirth and the festival offering.

Before the seder begins, a cup of wine is poured for the prophet Elijah, who is believed to visit every Jewish home on the night of the seder. During the seder meal, four cups of wine are drunk to commemorate four verbs used in the act of redemption. The youngest person at the seder asks four questions about Passover, which are then answered by the seder's leader. It is also customary for each person at the seder to dip his or her little finger into the wine to symbolize the ten plagues sent by God to the Egyptians to show His wrath for their refusal to release the children of Israel from bondage.

One favorite Passover custom is to hide the afikomen, half of one piece of the matzoh set aside before the seder. Children look for the piece of unleavened bread after the seder and are given a little prize, with a special gift awarded to the child who finds the afikomen. The afikomen is then shared among everyone at the seder table, the last thing eaten, to symbolize the inner life of each individual.

Matzoh Balls

2 eggs
2 tablespoons corn oil
2 tablespoons water

½ cup matzoh meal
dash coarsely ground black pepper

In medium bowl, beat eggs slightly. Stir in corn oil and water. Add matzoh meal and pepper, blending well. Cover and refrigerate 20 minutes. Meanwhile, in large kettle, bring 4 quarts water to boil. Reduce heat, allowing water to maintain a soft boil. Shape matzoh mixture into small balls and drop into boiling water. Reduce heat to medium low and cover. Cook 30 minutes. Use in chicken soup or as desired. Makes about 8 balls.

Charoset
....

1 medium apple, peeled and
    finely chopped
½ cup finely chopped walnuts
¼ cup chopped dates

½ teaspoon cinnamon
2 tablespoons sweet grape
    wine
2 tablespoons honey

In medium bowl, toss together apple, walnuts, dates, and cinnamon. Add wine and honey, mixing well. Makes about 1¼ cups.

SHAVUOT

Seven weeks after Passover, the Jewish people celebrate the two-day Shavuot, the third religious festival of the year. It commemorates the giving of the Ten Commandments (or Torah) on Mount Sinai and is tied to the harvest or "festival of firstfruits." Two sacrifices are made during Shavuot: two loaves of bread and various offerings of wheat, barley, olives, grapes, and such, to symbolize the firstfruits of the harvest.

The usual custom is to eat dairy products during Shavuot to represent nourishment received from milk and honey and from the dictates of the Torah. Cheesecake is one of the most popular dishes for the meal. Meat is forbidden, since it would remind Jews of the golden calf that led to the breaking of the Ten Commandments.

Shavuot Cheesecake

1¼ cups graham cracker crumbs
¼ cup sugar
⅓ cup melted butter
3 packages (8 ounces each)
    cream cheese
1 cup sugar

2 teaspoons vanilla extract
3 eggs
1 cup sour cream
sweetened whipped cream
    (optional)

In small bowl, combine graham cracker crumbs and ¼ cup sugar. Stir in melted butter. Press onto bottom and about halfway up sides of 9-inch springform pan. Cover and refrigerate while preparing filling. In large bowl, beat cream cheese until softened. Add 1 cup sugar and vanilla extract, beating well. Add eggs one at a time, beating well after each addition. Blend in sour cream. Pour into crust. Bake at 350 degrees for 1 hour. Turn off oven. Let cheesecake stand in oven 1 more hour. Cool completely on wire rack. Cover and refrigerate several hours or overnight. If desired, garnish with sweetened whipped cream just before serving. Makes 10 to 12 servings.

HANUKKAH

The Jewish "festival of lights" called Hanukkah (also spelled Chanukah) celebrates the triumph of the Jewish people over Greek values some twenty-one centuries ago. It was then that Judas Maccabeus and his soldiers ran the Syrians from the Temple in Jerusalem. The victorious troops thought they had just enough sanctified oil to keep the eternal flame lit for a single day, but by some miracle, the flame remained lit for eight days.

Today, Jews remember the miracle during December by lighting menorah candles for eight days, exchanging gifts, visiting with friends and family, and, of course, eating. During Hanukkah, it's traditional to eat dairy foods and use oil in cooking. Potato latkes are a "given" at the holiday table.

Potato Latkes

3 cups peeled and grated
  baking potatoes
⅓ cup all-purpose flour
1 egg, slightly beaten
1 tablespoon freshly grated onion

¼ teaspoon salt
dash coarsely ground black
  pepper
vegetable oil
applesauce and sour cream

Squeeze small amount of moisture from the grated potatoes using clean paper towels. Toss with flour, egg, onion, salt, and pepper, blending well. In large skillet, pour just enough oil to coat bottom. Heat over medium high heat. Drop ¼ cup of potato mixture onto hot oil. Fry until browned. Turn, flatten, and fry until other side is browned. Transfer to paper-towel-lined plate to drain. Cover and keep warm. Repeat frying procedure until all latkes are cooked, adding oil to skillet as needed. Serve with applesauce and sour cream. Makes 4 to 6 servings.

There are many other Jewish holidays with strong religious ties, strong traditions, and wonderful stories behind them. To learn more about Jewish customs, recipes, and crafts, I recommend *Celebrating the Jewish Holidays*, by Kalman, Levinrad, and Hirsch (Crescent Books, 1992).

So where do you go to experience kosher foods and celebration throughout the year? Many Jewish temples and nonprofit organizations offer food-oriented festivals, and I was able to find some right here in Pennsylvania.

The Jewish Federation of Greater Philadelphia does a good job with its Jewish Heritage Festival. This is a busy event with lots of activities to meet just about everyone's needs and likes. There's a telethon—the Allied Jewish Appeal Campaign—during the festival to raise funds for various causes within the Jewish community. Many use the event as an opportunity for reunions with friends and family, and the entertainment includes film and slide shows of old-time Jewish neighborhoods so visitors can reminisce about the old days. Children can busy themselves with crafts. Sometimes the kids make tzedakah, a charity box decorated with glitter and customized glue-ons, then use the box to collect money for charity.

The festival is also a delicious food bazaar. Professional caterers prepare quite a nice spread, usually vegetarian and always kosher. As a result, meat and dairy products are not served or eaten together, and all dishes are prepared in strict accordance with the rules of kosher food preparation.

Dishes include vegetarian tacos, tuna and egg salads, pasta, and confections. Vegetable-stuffed pastries called borekas are filling and satisfying. So is the baba ghannouj, an eggplant dip laced with garlic, and the tabbouleh, a classic Middle Eastern mixture of bulgur and fresh seasonings. If the weather is fine, you can enjoy falafel from the vendor outdoors. Falafel is a spicy garbanzo bean (chick pea) mixture that's fried and stuffed into pita bread and is usually topped with shredded greens and a sesame seed sauce (tahini).

About 3,000 people visit Philadelphia's Jewish Heritage Festival. It's geared to highlight a different Philadelphia-area Jewish community center, day school, or synagogue each year, and as a result, the location changes from one year to the next. There is no admission fee, parking is free, and prices for food and craft items are very reasonable. The event is usually held on a Sunday in April or May, but the date varies from year to year. For information on exact dates and locations, call the Jewish Federation of Greater Philadelphia at (215) 893-5600.

Sesame Tahini

1 cup raw sesame seeds   4 teaspoons vegetable oil

Sprinkle sesame seeds in large skillet. Heat over low heat, stirring constantly. Roast 10 to 15 minutes, stirring and shaking pan frequently, or until lightly browned and fragrant. Place in food processor with oil. Process on high speed until smooth and consistency of peanut butter. Store in a cool, dry place. Makes about 1 cup.

Baba Ghannouj

1 medium eggplant
¼ cup fresh lemon juice
2 cloves garlic, crushed
1 teaspoon salt

3 tablespoons sesame tahini
extra-virgin olive oil
ground cumin
warm pita bread wedges

Place eggplant on baking sheet. Bake at 375 degrees for 45 minutes, or until very tender. Let stand until cool enough to handle. Peel and chop fine. In large, shallow bowl, combine eggplant, lemon juice, garlic, and salt. Beat in tahini with fork until blended and smooth. Let stand at room temperature about 30 minutes to blend flavors. Drizzle with olive oil and cumin. Serve with warm pita bread wedges for dipping. Makes 4 servings.

Tabbouleh

1 cup bulgur wheat, rinsed
  and drained
⅓ cup fresh lemon juice
1 teaspoon salt
⅛ teaspoon coarsely ground
  black pepper
⅔ cup extra-virgin olive oil
½ cup snipped fresh parsley

½ cup thinly sliced green
  onions
⅓ cup snipped fresh mint
  leaves
1 medium tomato,
  chopped
romaine lettuce leaves

In medium bowl, cover bulgur with cold water. Let stand 1 hour at room temperature. Drain well and squeeze out excess moisture. In separate large bowl, combine lemon juice, salt, and pepper. Gradually whisk in olive oil, blending well. Add drained bulgur, parsley, green onions, and mint, tossing lightly. Cover and refrigerate at least 2 hours before serving. Spoon onto salad plates. Sprinkle with tomato. Surround with romaine lettuce leaves. Serve immediately. Makes 4 to 6 servings.

The Bucks County region of Greater Philadelphia's Jewish Federation puts on its own Jewish Community Festival every year as "a way to bring together the community in a celebration of Jewish life." Area synagogues and community-service organizations support the event, providing lots to see and do.

The Bucks County event is youth-oriented, with lots of hands-on activities. Kids can participate in the "make and take" craft project, which usually involves making a kippah, the traditional Jewish head covering. Young crafters are then seen proudly wearing their creations. Children's choral groups and bands perform, and most kids participate in the ethnic sing-alongs and folk dancing.

Crafts are sold at the Bucks County festival and include a variety of Jewish ceremonial items, such as hanukkah candles and seder plates and original artwork. The festival is also a charitable event, raising funds and gathering food and clothing for the needy. Guests are encouraged to visit every synagogue booth at the festival and receive information on a different Jewish holiday at each.

The congregation from each of Bucks County's fifteen synagogues prepares food for the festival, and everything is kosher. There's falafel, tahini, and hummus at this event, as well as knishes (wonderful little baked pastries stuffed with potato, liver, or vegetables), a noodle pudding called kugel, and sweet baked goods like schnecken, a tender pastry filled with nuts and raisins.

The Bucks County region of Greater Philadelphia's Jewish Federation holds its annual Jewish Festival on one Sunday in June at the Middletown Grange Fair Grounds in Wrightstown. For more information, call the Jewish Federation of Greater Philadelphia, Bucks County Region, at (215) 579-9300.

Kugel

1 box matzoh farfel
(16-ounce size)
2½ cups hot chicken broth
or stock
1 cup butter, divided
1 large onion, finely chopped
1 cup sliced fresh mushrooms
1 cup chopped celery

½ cup chopped green bell
pepper
2 eggs, slightly beaten
1 tablespoon snipped fresh
parsley
¼ teaspoon ground ginger
salt and coarsely ground
black pepper, to taste

In large bowl, soak farfel in chicken broth or stock. Meanwhile, melt ½ cup of the butter in large skillet. Add onion, mushrooms, celery, and bell pepper and sauté until lightly browned. Melt remaining ½ cup butter and add to soaked farfel mixture. Stir in sautéed vegetables, eggs, parsley, ginger, salt, and pepper. Spoon into well-greased 13×11-inch baking pan. Bake at 375 degrees for 1 hour, or until lightly browned and crisp. Serve hot. Makes 10 to 12 servings.

The Jewish Community Center of Chester and Delaware Counties puts on a large Jewish Festival in Valley Forge each fall, joining forces with six area synagogues to offer their own "celebration of Jewish life." For about $5, visitors gobble up the falafel, deli sandwiches, and kosher hot dogs in an informal atmosphere of Israeli dancing, choral groups, Middle Eastern music, and cultural information. Those with a sweet tooth just love the Jewish apple cake and cheese Danish, too, and there are plenty of bagels in various flavors to eat there or take home for a quick breakfast or snack.

The Jewish Festival of Chester and Delaware Counties is held one Sunday in September or October at the Valley Forge Convention Center near Philadelphia. (Avid shoppers should make a side trip to the King of Prussia Mall just down the road.) For more information, call (610) 356-9850.

Falafel

3 cups cooked garbanzo beans
  (chick peas), drained
  and ground
2 eggs, slightly beaten
2 tablespoons wheat germ
1 tablespoon snipped fresh parsley
1 clove garlic, minced
1 teaspoon salt

⅛ teaspoon cayenne
  (ground red pepper)
vegetable oil
pita bread halves
shredded lettuce
Sesame Tahini
  (see page 168)

In large bowl, combine ground garbanzo beans, eggs, wheat germ, parsley, garlic, salt, and cayenne. Shape into 1-inch balls. Flatten slightly. In large skillet, pour oil to depth of about ½ inch. Heat oil over medium high heat. Fry balls, a few at a time, in hot oil until crisp. Remove from oil and transfer to paper-towel-lined plate to drain. Keep warm while frying remaining falafel. Then stuff into pita halves and top with shredded lettuce and Sesame Tahini. Makes 4 to 6 servings.

The Sinai Temple in the Squirrel Hill area just outside Pittsburgh holds a three-day Jewish Food Festival each November. Close to 1,000 people come to enjoy kosher dishes like potato latkes, cheese blintzes, stuffed cabbage, cabbage and noodles, corned beef, chicken, and hot dogs. Temple volunteers prepare and serve the reasonably priced dishes. Profits benefit causes of the Sinai Temple, located at 5505 Forbes Ave., Pittsburgh, PA 15217. For more information, call (412) 421-9715.

Cheese Blintzes

3 eggs
¼ cup milk
¼ cup water
⅓ cup unbleached all-purpose
flour

about 2 tablespoons
butter, divided
cheese filling (below)
applesauce or fresh fruit
puree

In small bowl, beat eggs well using a wire whisk or fork. Add milk and water, beating well. Gradually add flour, beating with a wooden spoon until blended and smooth. Heat a crepe pan or small skillet, and melt 1 teaspoon of the butter over medium heat.

Add about 2 tablespoons of the batter, tilting pan to coat bottom. Heat until batter begins to set and edge curls away from side of pan. Invert onto paper-towel-lined surface. Repeat cooking procedure with remaining batter, using additional butter in pan, as needed. Place crepe on plate, cooked side up. Spoon generous tablespoonful of cheese filling onto center. Fold opposite sides over filling. Fold two remaining sides up and over. Repeat filling and folding with remaining crepes and filling. In large skillet, melt 1 tablespoon butter over medium heat. Add blintzes and sauté until golden brown on both sides, turning once during cooking. Serve immediately with applesauce or fresh fruit puree. Makes about 1 dozen.

Cheese Filling: Drain excess liquid from 2 cups dry, small curd cottage cheese. In medium bowl, combine cottage cheese and 2 tablespoons sugar. Cover and refrigerate until ready to use.

BAGELS

Bagels have become a very popular food for breakfast, snacking, and sandwiches. That's good, because bagels are high in complex carbohydrates and low in fat. (At last, something that really tastes good and that's good for us, too.)

Most connoisseurs describe the optimum bagel as crusty on the outside, soft on the inside, and chewy without being stale. You should be able to see some irregular holes and little craters when the bagel is cut in half. (Be careful—hospital emergency rooms see wounded bagel slicers on a regular basis. For safest handling, buy a device for holding the bagel from a kitchen equipment shop.)

Let's face it—nobody in their right mind makes bagels from scratch anymore . . . well, maybe Martha Stewart. The rest of us go to the nearest bagel shop when we're in the mood for the real thing.

The New York Bagel Bakery in West Philadelphia makes the very best, in about fifteen flavors, including the classic plain, poppy seed, cinnamon-raisin, and chocolate chip. The bakers have decades of bagel-baking experience and, as a result, know their craft. They boast an authentic bagel-making process, which includes mixing the dough from scratch, allowing it to rise, shaping it, then boiling and baking the bagels on a daily basis.

The New York Bagel Bakery opened in 1962 and is kosher. It's located at 7555 Haverford Rd., Philadelphia, PA 19151, telephone (215) 878-8080. The shop is open seven days a week starting at 6:00 A.M.

If you're looking for something more than bagels, try Gerard's, a Jewish delicatessen located in lower Bucks County. The store carries plenty of specialty foods, including deli meats prepared by a full-service butcher, an assortment of cheese, whitefish salad, a zesty dilled tuna salad, and baked goodies galore. Gerard's will cater your event, too, with menus to fit various Jewish holidays.

Gerard's is located at 265 Second St. Pike on Route 232 in Southampton, PA 18966, telephone (215) 355-6180. It's open seven days a week from 8:00 A.M., with various afternoon or evening closing times.

Mexico

Keystone Fiestas and Siestas

Pennsylvania may not have a huge Mexican population, but the state's growing love affair with Mexican cuisine has led to a surge in Mexican restaurants and interest in cooking Mexican at home.

The basic diet of Mexico's natives hasn't changed much since the beginning of recorded time. Corn, beans, tomatoes, and squash have been the mainstays of the Mexican diet for centuries. Meats remain seasoned with hot chilies and then rotisseried. Tamales and tortillas have outlived the generations, along with cinnamon-spiced chocolate drinks and a fermented beverage called octli.

When Spaniards arrived in Mexico in the 1500s, they added pork, beef, rice, and spices such as cumin to the Mexican menu. The Spaniards also introduced olive oil, garbanzo beans, codfish, olives, almonds, and honey, popular ingredients in Mexican dishes today.

And Mexican food here in the United States has gone far beyond tacos. (In Mexico, a taco is anything wrapped in a tortilla, just as a sandwich here in the States is anything consisting of two slices of bread and filling between them.) True Mexican recipes are more unique, upscale, and varied than what we experience in those national chain restaurants. More and more, we see mom and pop restaurants reflecting the true variety of ingredients and techniques used in Mexican homes.

If you want to try truly authentic and somewhat upscale Mexican recipes at home, get *Mexico's Feasts of Life*, by Patricia Quintana (Council Oaks Books, 1994). For classic southwestern recipes, clearly explained, see Lisa Golden Schroeder's *Sizzling Southwestern Cookery* (Meadowbrook Press, 1989).

A GLOSSARY OF
MEXICAN INGREDIENTS

achiote: reddish brown seeds that are boiled in water to make a yellow food coloring for sauces and rice

azafrán: Mexican version of saffron

chilies: category of hot, spicy peppers commonly used in Mexican dishes; some typical mild variations include chilaca, poblano, serrano, and jalapeño; hot varieties include güero, habanero, and manzano

chipotles: smoked jalapeño peppers

chocolate: Mexican versions are usually bitter and sold in cakes

epazote: a rare Mexican herb; sage may be substituted

guayabate: sweet paste made from guavas, served on slices of mild cheese as dessert

harina: all-purpose flour

Jamaica: maroon-colored flower dried and used to make a sweet drink similar to cranberry in flavor

jicama: dull-colored root similar to a potato in appearance; tastes similar to water chestnuts

lard: rendered hog fat, used as the fat in many Mexican dishes; solid vegetable shortening may be substituted

manzanilla: dried flowers used to brew tea

masa: moist dough made from dried corn that has been soaked in limewater and cooked; instant version is available in the United States

mole: rich meat sauce made with chilies, various spices, and usually chocolate

nopales: pads of the pear cactus; used in soups, salads, omelets, or alone

piloncillo (panocha): unrefined brown cane sugar used to sweeten coffee and desserts

piñones: pine nuts

pipián: variation of mole thickened with sesame or pumpkin seeds

queso: mild, white Mexican cheese

salsa: general term for Mexican sauces used in and on various dishes; usually composed of tomatoes, chilies, herbs, and other seasonings

tomatillo: small, sweet, green tomato with lemony flavor; used in sauces

One of my favorite local Harrisburg Mexican restaurants, El Rodeo, is family owned and operated. It's intimate and informal, with an old, dark, polished bar and frozen margaritas that sneak up on you. The menu isn't fancy but is appealing to those who want real Mexican food at reasonable prices. Meals start with fresh-baked tortilla chips and a medium hot salsa. The main course portions are large and include chicken chimichangas, shredded, marinated chicken wrapped in soft or fried flour tortillas and topped with an understated guacamole; steak fajitas, tender slices of beef stir-fried with bell pepper, onion, and tomatoes; and of course, tacos. Most entrées are topped with plenty of guacamole and sour cream and come with a side of refried beans lightly sprinkled with shredded cheddar.

El Rodeo's prices range from about $6 for most house specialties to about $10 for steak entrées. Food is prepared fresh to order and comes to your table piping hot. The restaurant is open seven days a week and does not accept reservations. El Rodeo is located at 4659 Jonestown Rd. in Harrisburg, telephone (717) 652-5340, and has a second location at 724 Louck Rd. in York, telephone (717) 845-1341.

Chimichangas

....

10 flour tortillas (below)
1½ tablespoons vegetable oil
1 medium onion, chopped
1 cup chopped tomato
2 cups shredded cooked chicken
1 can diced green chilies
    (4-ounce size), drained
salt and coarsely ground black
    pepper, to taste

2 cups shredded cheddar
    cheeese
additional vegetable oil
    (optional)
guacamole
    (recipe follows)
sour cream

Prepare flour tortillas and keep warm. In large skillet, heat oil
over medium heat. Add onion and tomato, and sauté for 3 minutes.
Drain off any excess liquid. Stir in chicken and chilies. Heat
through. Salt and pepper to taste. Spoon 2 generous tablespoonfuls
in center of each tortilla. Top with cheese. Wrap tortilla around
filling. Serve immediately, or if desired, fry in hot vegetable oil
until lightly browned. Top with guacamole and sour cream before
serving. Makes 10.

Flour Tortillas: In food processor, combine 3 cups all-purpose
flour, ¼ cup solid vegetable shortening, and ½ teaspoon salt.
Process until consistency of cornmeal. Add water and process
5 seconds, or just until dough forms. Knead dough on lightly
floured surface 3 to 4 minutes. Cover with damp cloth and let
stand 30 minutes. Divide dough into 10 equal portions. Shape
into balls. Using rolling pin, roll out each ball to 7-inch-diameter
round between two pieces of waxed paper. Preheat large,
ungreased skillet over medium heat. Remove top layer of waxed
paper from one of the tortillas and invert into hot skillet.
Peel off remaining waxed paper. Heat until bottom is lightly
browned. Turn and continue heating until other side is
lightly browned. Repeat cooking procedure with remaining
tortillas. Wrap in foil and keep warm in 250-degree oven until
ready to use. Makes 10.

Guacamole

2 large ripe avocados, peeled,
   pitted, and chopped
2 tablespoons fresh lime juice

½ teaspoon salt
2 tablespoons snipped
   fresh cilantro (optional)

Mash avocados with potato masher or fork. Blend in lime juice
and salt. Stir in cilantro, if desired. Serve with tortilla chips
or as a topping for Mexican dishes. Makes about 2 cups.

Trendy chefs are appalled to think that tacos and guacamole are the be-
all and end-all Mexican dishes in the minds of Pennsylvanians. As a
result, culinary experts strive to expose Keystone Staters to a greater
variety of authentic dishes. Michele Leff and partner David Fetkewick
are doing just that at their West Philadelphia restaurant Zocalo.

Zocalo is stylish, comfortable, and quaint, with a series of cozy dining
rooms and sculpted white walls donned with neoprimitive paintings.
All food is made to order. Fresh chilies are soaked and pureed every
Saturday to use in dishes the following week. Zocalo's offerings include
duck in Oaxacan mole (Oaxaca is a region in southern Mexico), sword-
fish tacos (wrapped with handmade tortillas), and dishes grilled at your
table. Dessert options include an unusual but deliciously spiced ice
cream sandwich with pumpkin seeds and habanero chilies, sweet
tamales, chocolate cactus in meringue, and a margarita cake flavored
with fresh lime.

Zocalo is located at 36th Street and Lancaster Avenue on the
Drexel University campus in Philadelphia and is open Monday through
Saturday. Three-course dinners cost about $13.95. Phone (215) 895-
0139 for more information and reservations.

Mole de Guajolote
(Turkey Mole)

12-pound fresh turkey, cut up
½ cup all-purpose flour
1 tablespoon salt, divided
½ cup shortening
2 large onions, chopped
1 can tomato sauce (8-ounce size)
¾ cup chili powder
½ cup natural peanut butter
½ cup raisins
2 squares (2 ounces) unsweetened baking chocolate, chopped
1 clove garlic, minced
¼ teaspoon ground anise
¼ teaspoon ground coriander
¼ teaspoon ground cumin
¼ teaspoon ground cloves
2 slices white bread, toasted
4 corn tortillas, toasted
2 tablespoons toasted sesame seeds
6 cups stock from cooked turkey
1 tablespoon sugar
hot cooked white rice

Rub turkey with flour mixed with 1 teaspoon of the salt. In large skillet, melt shortening over medium heat. Add turkey and brown on all sides. Transfer to Dutch oven or large kettle. Cover with cold water. Add remaining 2 teaspoons salt. Cover and bring to boil. Reduce heat and simmer 3 hours, or until turkey is very tender and cooked through. Remove turkey from Dutch oven, reserving stock. Cool turkey, then remove skin, bones, neck, and other portions of carcass and return to stock. Cover and continue cooking 1 hour. Meanwhile, coarsely chop turkey meat. Set aside. Add onions to skillet used for browning turkey. Sauté 5 minutes over medium high heat, or until onions are lightly browned. Stir in tomato sauce, chili powder, peanut butter, raisins, chocolate, garlic, anise, coriander, cumin, and cloves. Tear bread and tortillas into pieces, and stir into tomato mixture with sesame seeds and 2 cups of the turkey stock. Transfer to food processor. Process until smooth. Transfer to large saucepan. Add 4 cups additional turkey stock and the sugar. Stir in turkey meat. Heat through. Serve over hot rice. Makes 10 to 12 servings.

Zocalo's owners also own and operate the 12th Street Cantina and Cantina on Main, Mexican specialty stores with quite a following. Michele explains that there was nothing close to a Mexican gourmet market in the Philadelphia area, so she and David jumped at the opportunity to fill a niche. Both Cantinas offer a full-service Mexican deli and plethora of fresh, dried, and imported chilies and powders. You can buy homemade tortillas, chips, and salsa in unique flavors like mango-tomatillo and roasted pepper. Many products are packaged under the Cantina label.

Both Cantinas serve lunch, too, and the menu includes trendy items such as grilled vegetables in roasted garlic and corn, and wild mushroom enchiladas in chili cream sauce. If you're in a hurry, select heat-and-serve entrées from the display case to take home and eat later. The reasonably priced dishes change often.

The 12th Street Cantina is located at 12th and Arch Streets in the Reading Terminal Market, and Cantina on Main is located at 4120 Main St. in the Manayunk Farmers Market, both in Philadelphia. Call (215) 625-0321 for more information on available products, as well as days and hours of operation for either location.

Santa Fe Salsa

4 medium tomatoes, diced
8 green onions, minced
1 medium onion, chopped
1 ripe avocado, peeled, pitted, and diced
½ cup snipped fresh cilantro

2 fresh jalapeño peppers, minced
⅓ cup fresh lime juice
1 teaspoon snipped fresh oregano
salt and coarsely ground black pepper, to taste

In large bowl, combine all ingredients. Cover and refrigerate until ready to serve. If made several hours in advance, add avocado just before serving. Use as a dip for tortilla chips or as a sauce for Mexican foods. Makes 6 to 8 servings.

To learn how to cook Mexican at home, head to The Kitchen Shoppe and Cooking School in Carlisle. The Kitchen Shoppe has many first-rate, nationally known teachers who demonstrate unusual cooking techniques and ingredients for their students. The Shoppe carries every imaginable kitchen gadget, as well as cookbooks, linens, fine china, and stoneware. Instructor and food writer Diana Povis is the resident expert on Mexican cuisine. She teaches a variety of classes covering just about every south-of-the-border culinary technique, including smoked foods, upscale ideas, and hands-on taco instruction for kids.

One unusual Mexican dish, an appetizer called pumpkin tamales with spiced butter, consists of a pumpkin puree flavored with honey, ginger, cinnamon, and nutmeg, then steamed inside corn husks and served hot. Ancho pepper–rubbed chicken is grilled and served with a cranberry-apricot relish. Sweet potato and chipotle gratin relies on smoked jalapeño peppers for its flavor. Diana's chocolate polenta soufflé cake is a rich and curious finale to one of her Mexican cooking class meals.

The Kitchen Shoppe is owned and operated by Suzanne Hoffman and is located at 101 Shady Lane, Carlisle, PA 17013. For information on available products, classes, and specific hours of operation, call (717) 243-0906.

Corn Salad–Stuffed Artichokes

2 packages frozen corn kernels
 (10-ounce size)
¾ cup sliced, cooked carrots
⅔ cup chopped green
 bell pepper
½ cup mayonnaise
2 tablespoons grated fresh onion
1 teaspoon chili powder
⅛ teaspoon salt
⅛ teaspoon coarsely
 ground black pepper
6 fresh artichokes
chili mayonnaise (below)

Cook corn according to package directions. Drain and cool. Place in large bowl. Add carrots, bell pepper, mayonnaise, onion, chili powder, salt, and pepper. Gently toss to combine. Cover and refrigerate at least 1 hour to blend flavors. Remove stems from artichokes. Using kitchen shears, snip about ½ inch from tips of leaves. Drop artichokes into lightly salted, boiling water. Cover and cook 45 minutes. Drain and shake to remove excess moisture. Cool to room temperature. Gently tap artichokes on countertop to spread leaves. Cover and refrigerate until chilled. Stuff with corn mixture. Arrange on serving platter. Serve with chili mayonnaise. Makes 6 servings.

Chili Mayonnaise: In small bowl, combine 1 cup mayonnaise, 1 tablespoon fresh lemon juice, 1 teaspoon chili powder, ½ teaspoon salt, and dash coarsely ground black pepper. Cover and refrigerate until ready to serve.

CINCO DE MAYO

Cinco de Mayo is Mexico's most widely celebrated holiday, held to commemorate the victory of Mexican troops over the invading French army on May 5, 1862. Hispanics here in the States also observe the holiday, with parades, parties, and feasts to strengthen ethnic ties and raise awareness about the Hispanic community. The following are some holiday recipes for your own Cinco de Mayo celebration.

Garlic-Tomato Soup

4 large tomatoes, coarsely chopped
⅓ cup butter
⅓ cup olive oil
3 heads (bulbs) garlic, cloves peeled and minced
14 cups beef broth or stock
salt and coarsely ground black pepper, to taste

⅓ cup snipped fresh cilantro
2 eggs, slightly beaten
1 cup crumbled feta cheese
1 fresh jalapeño pepper, minced
croutons

Puree tomatoes in food processor. Strain lightly and set aside. In large saucepan, melt butter with olive oil over medium high heat. Add garlic, and sauté just until very lightly browned. Reduce heat to medium. Add tomato puree. Cook and stir until thickened. Add beef broth or stock. Cook 20 minutes. Salt and pepper to taste. Stir in cilantro. Bring to boil. Gradually add eggs, stirring or whisking constantly. Stir in cheese and jalapeño pepper. Heat through. Serve hot with croutons. Makes 6 to 8 servings.

Refried Beans

1 pound dry pinto beans,
   rinsed and drained
cold water to cover
5 cups water

1 large onion, diced
½ cup melted butter
salt, to taste
shredded cheddar cheese

Cover beans with cold water. Cover and soak overnight in refrigerator. Drain and rinse. Drain again. In large kettle, combine soaked beans, 5 cups water, and onion. Cover and bring to boil. Reduce heat and simmer, covered, for 3 hours, or until very tender. Mash with potato masher or fork. Add melted butter. Cook and stir over low heat until mixture is combined and thickened. Salt to taste. Serve hot, sprinkled with shredded cheddar cheese. Makes 6 to 8 servings.

Crema de Mango
(Mango Cream)

5 large, ripe, fresh mangoes,
   peeled, seeded, and chopped
sugar, to taste
2 oranges, peeled, seeded,
   and chopped
1 tablespoon fresh lemon juice

2 cups heavy or whipping
   cream
1 cup chopped pecans
8 to 10 well-drained
   maraschino cherries

In large bowl or food processor, mash mangoes. Add sugar to desired sweetness. Stir in oranges and lemon juice. Whip cream until soft peaks form. Fold whipped cream and pecans into fruit mixture. Spoon into dessert dishes. Garnish with maraschino cherries. Serve immediately or refrigerate until ready to serve. Makes 8 to 10 servings.

Spirited Beef

1 tablespoon butter
1 large onion, chopped
1 green bell pepper, chopped
1 red bell pepper, chopped
½ cup hot beef bouillon
2 tablespoons tomato paste
¾ teaspoon salt, divided
⅛ teaspoon coarsely ground
    black pepper

4 drops hot pepper sauce
4 rib eye steaks, 4 to
    6 ounces each
coarsely ground black
    pepper, to taste
2 tablespoons vegetable oil
2 tablespoons tequila
⅛ teaspoon cayenne
    (ground red pepper)

In large skillet, melt butter over medium high heat. Add onion, and sauté until lightly browned. Add green and red bell peppers. Sauté 2 more minutes. Remove from heat. In small bowl, combine hot beef bouillon and tomato paste. Add to sautéed vegetables. Stir in ½ teaspoon of the salt, ⅛ teaspoon pepper, and hot sauce. Place over medium heat. Cover and simmer 10 minutes, stirring occasionally. Pat meat dry with paper towels. Rub with pepper to taste. In large skillet, heat oil over medium high heat. Add meat. Cook 3 minutes on each side, or to desired doneness. Arrange vegetable mixture on large, heated serving platter. Top with meat. To drippings in skillet, add tequila, cayenne, and remaining ¼ teaspoon salt. Use spoon to scrape down any brown bits from side of skillet, stirring into mixture. Heat through. Spoon over meat and vegetables. Serve immediately. Makes 4 servings.

Ethnic Food Events

Many of Pennsylvania's ethnic food events are listed below. However, they are subject to change from one year to the next, so call ahead to confirm locations, dates, and times as well as other information.

FEBRUARY
Mardi Gras Ball, Philadelphia
Alliance Française de
  Philadelphia
(215) 735-5283

Chinese New Year Banquets,
  Philadelphia
Chinese Cultural and
  Community Center
(215) 923-6767 or -6768
  (through April)

A Soul Food Sampling,
  Alison Park (Pittsburgh)
North Area YWCA
(412) 366-4381

Greater Philadelphia Scottish
  & Irish Festival, Valley Forge
East of the Hebrides
  Entertainments
(610) 825-7268

MARCH
Irish Extravaganza, Pocono
  Manor
Pocono Manor Inn and Golf
  Resort
(800) 233-8150

APRIL
Jewish Heritage Festival,
  Philadelphia
Jewish Federation of Greater
  Philadelphia
(215) 893-5640

MAY
St. Nicholas Greek Food
  Festival, Pittsburgh
St. Nicholas Cathedral
(412) 682-3866

Capital Region Greek Festival,
  Wormleysburg
Holy Trinity Greek Orthodox
  Cathedral
(717) 763-7441

Spring Highlands Festival,
    Edinboro
Edinboro University
(800) 526-0121 or
    (814) 732-2672

Italian Market Festival,
    Philadelphia
Philadelphia Convention and
    Visitors Bureau
(800) 537-7676 or
    (215) 636-1666

Ukrainian Summer Activities,
    Lehighton
Ukrainian Homestead
(610) 377-4621 or
    (215) 235-3709
    (through Labor Day)

Pocono's Greatest Irish Festival,
    Blakeslee
Jack Frost Mountain
(800) 468-2442 or
    (717) 443-8425

JUNE
Pennsylvania Dutch Food
    Festival, Lancaster (several
    locations)
Pennsylvania Dutch
    Convention and Visitors
    Bureau
(800) PA DUTCH or
    (717) 299-8901

Food, Farm and Fun Fest,
    Lancaster
Artworks Expo Center
(717) 738-9500 or -9503

French Azilum Tours, Towanda
French Azilum
(717) 265-3376 (through August)

African Family Festival,
    Harrisburg
Ngozi, Inc.
(717) 234-7724

Delco Scottish Games, Media
East of the Hebrides
    Entertainments
(610) 825-7268 or -4381

Jewish Community Festival,
    Wrightstown
Jewish Federation of Greater
    Philadelphia—Bucks County
    Region
(215) 579-9300

Traditional American Indian
    Pow-Wow, Forksville
Eastern Delaware Nations
(717) 928-9259 or
    (717) 836-5431

Jim Thorpe Memorial
    Pow-Wow, Carlisle
Carlisle Fairgrounds
(717) 243-7855, or Pow Wow,
    (919) 257-5383

JULY
Kutztown Folk Festival, Kutztown
Festival Associates
(610) 683-8707, or Kutztown
    Fairgrounds, (800) 963-8824

Bastille Day Celebration,
Philadelphia
Alliance Française de
Philadelphia
(215) 735-5283

AUGUST
Dankfest, Harmony
Harmony Museum
(412) 452-7341

The Pennsylvania Renaissance
Faire, Cornwall
(717) 665-7021 (through
mid-October)

African American Heritage
Project of Blair County,
Altoona
Railroader's Memorial Museum
(814) 946-0834

African American
Extravaganza, Philadelphia
Penn's Landing
(215) 457-4725

La Festa Italiana, Scranton
La Festa Committee
(717) 344-7411 or
(717) 346-6384

SEPTEMBER
Italian Heritage Festival,
Reading
Italian Heritage Festival
(610) 929-2977

Lebanon Bologna Fest, Lebanon
Expo Center
(717) 656-3559

Seven Sweets & Sours,
Intercourse
Kitchen Kettle Village
(717) 768-8261

Oktoberfest, Pittsburgh
Penn Brewery
(412) 237-9402

Scottish Highland Games,
Ligonier
Idlewild Park
(412) 238-3666

Pittsburgh Irish Festival,
Pittsburgh
Pittsburgh Irish Festival, Inc.
(412) 422-5642

Celtic Classic Highland Games,
Bethlehem
Celtic Fest, Inc.
(610) 868-9599

Blands Park Italian Food
Festival, Tipton
Blands Park
(814) 684-3538

Jewish Festival of Chester and
Delaware Counties, Valley
Forge
Chester and Delaware County
Region of Jewish Community
Centers
(610) 356-9850

Native American Festival at
Wildcat Park, Ludlow
Festival Coordinators
(814) 362-4068 or
(814) 368-9370

Shawnee Mountain Scottish
and Irish Games and Music
Festival, Shawnee-on-
Delaware
Shawnee Mountain Ski Area
(717) 421-7231

Mountain Top Pow Wow,
Mountain Top
Native American Association
(717) 226-2620

Ukrainian Renaissance Festival,
Pittsburgh
Nationality Room Program @
Cathedral of Learning
(412) 624-6000

OCTOBER
Springs Folk Festival, Salisbury
Festival Coordinators
(814) 662-4158 or
(814) 662-2051

Greek Food Bazaar, Reading
Saints Constantine and Helen
Greek Orthodox Church
(610) 374-7511

Manor College Ukrainian
Festival, Jenkintown
Manor College
(215) 885-2360

NOVEMBER
Christkindlmarkt, Bethlehem
Musikfest Association
(610) 861-0678 (through
Christmas)

Divali, New Cumberland
American Religious Institute
(717) 774-7750

Divali, Wilkes Barre
Indo-American Association of
Northeast Pennsylvania
(717) 825-5510

Jewish Food Festival, Pittsburgh
Sinai Temple
(412) 421-9715

Irish Extravaganza, Pocono
Manor
Pocono Manor Inn and
Golf Resort
(800) 233-8150

DECEMBER
Christkindlmarkt, Hershey
Hershey Museum
(717) 534-3439

Kwanzaa Festival, Harrisburg
Harrisburg Area Community
College
(717) 780-2632

Kwanzaa Festival, Shippensburg
Shippensburg University
(717) 532-1616

APPENDIX B

Selected
Ethnic Restaurants

ITALIAN

Assaggi Italiani, 935 Ellsworth
St., Philadelphia
(215) 339-0700

Bistro Romano, 120 Lombard
St., Philadelphia
(215) 925-8880

Davio, 2100 Broadway Ave.,
Pittsburgh
(412) 531-7422

D'Angelos, 256 S. 20th St.,
Philadelphia
(215) 546-3935

Felicia's, 1148 S. 11th St.,
Philadelphia
(215) 755-9656

Frederick's, 757 S. Front St.,
Philadelphia
(215) 271-FRED

Joseph's, 1915 E. Passyunk Ave.,
Philadelphia
(215) 755-2770

La Collina, 37–41 Ashland Ave.,
Belmont Hills
(610) 668-1780

La Famiglia Ristorante,
8 S. Front St., Philadelphia
(215) 922-2803

La Vigna, 1100 S. Front St.,
Philadelphia
(215) 336-1100

Litto's Bakery & Cafe, 910
Christian St., Philadelphia
(215) 627-7037

Mr. Martino's Trattoria, 1646 E.
Passyunk Ave., Philadelphia
(215) 755-0663

Pietro's Italian Chophouse,
Hyatt Regency,
112 Washington Place at
Chatham Center, Pittsburgh
(412) 288-9326

Rillo's, 50 Pine St., Carlisle
(717) 766-8373 or
(717) 243-6141

FRENCH

Accomac Inn, Accomac Rd.,
Wrightsville
(717) 252-1521

Alisa Cafe, 109 Fairfield Ave.,
Upper Darby
(610) 352-4402

California Cafe, 52 W. Pomfret
St., Carlisle
(717) 249-2028

Chez Gerard, Rt. 40 East,
Hopewood
(412) 437-9001

Deux Cheminees, 1221 Locust
St., Philadelphia
(215) 790-0200

La Fourchette, 110 N. Wayne
Ave., Wayne
(610) 687-8333

La Truffe, 10 S. Front St.,
Philadelphia
(215) 925-5062

Le Bec-Fin, 1523 Walnut St.,
Philadelphia
(215) 567-1000

Le Pommier, 2104 E. Carson St.,
Pittsburgh
(412) 431-1901

Pat's Place, 1307 Airbrake Ave.,
Turtle Creek
(412) 829-7364

The Restaurant at Donecker's,
333 N. State St., Ephrata
(717) 738-9501

GERMAN AND
PENNSYLVANIA DUTCH

Amish Barn Restaurant, Rt. 340,
3029 Old Philadelphia Pike,
Bird-in-Hand
(717) 768-8886

Bird-in-Hand Family Restaurant,
Rt. 340, 2760 Old Philadelphia
Pike, Bird-in-Hand
(717) 768-8266

Dunderbak's, 121 Lehigh Valley
Mall, Whitehall
(610) 264-4963

Good & Plenty Restaurant,
Rt. 896, Smoketown
(717) 394-7111

Groff's Farm Restaurant,
650 Pinkerton Rd., Mt. Joy
(717) 653-2048

Intercourse Village Restaurant,
Rts. 340 & 772, Intercourse
(717) 768-3637

Kitchen Kettle Village, Rt. 340,
Intercourse
(717) 768-8261

Kleiner Deutschmann,
643 Pittsburgh St., Springdale
(412) 274-5022

Miller's County Fare Restaurant,
Rt. 30, 2811 Lincoln Highway
East, Ronks
(717) 687-6621

Otto's Brauhaus & Beer Garden,
233 Easton Rd., Horsham
(215) 675-1864

Penn Brewery, Troy Hill Rd. and
Vinial St., Pittsburgh
(412) 237-9402

Plain & Fancy Farm Restaurant,
Rt. 340, between Bird-in-
Hand and Intercourse
(717) 768-4400

Stoltzfus Farm Restaurant,
3716A E. Newport Rd.,
Intercourse
(717) 768-8156

Washington House Restaurant
& Pub, Rt. 896, Strasburg
(717) 687-9211 or
(800) 872-0201

Willow Valley Family Restaurant,
Rt. 222, Lancaster
(717) 464-2711

Zinn's Diner, Rt. 272, Denver
(717) 336-1774

POLISH

Warsaw Cafe, 306 S. 16th St.,
Philadelphia
(215) 546-0204

UKRAINIAN

Ulana's, 205 Bainbridge St.,
Philadelphia
(215) 922-4152

IRISH AND SCOTTISH

Annie's Cafe, 98 Cricket Ave.,
Ardmore
(610) 649-0283

Blarney Stone Restaurant,
30 Grant Ave., Pittsburgh
(412) 781-1666

Brittingham's Irish Pub,
640 Germantown Pike,
Lafayette Hill
(610) 828-7351

Byrne's Tavern, 3301 Richmond
St., Philadelphia
(215) 634-8707

Cawley's Restaurant & Tavern,
7819 West Chester Pike,
Upper Darby
(610) 789-0799

Coakley's Restaurant & Pub,
305 Bridge St.,
New Cumberland
(717) 774-5556

Fiddler's Green Dining House,
208 W. Beidler Rd.,
King of Prussia
(610) 337-3888

The Irish Bards, 2013 Walnut
St., Philadelphia
(215) 569-9585

McGillin's Olde Irish Ale House,
1310 Drury Lane, Philadelphia
(215) 735-5562

McGlinchey's, 19 E. State St.,
Doylestown
(215) 345-8181

Mick's Inn, 146 Bustleton Pike,
Feasterville
(215) 364-5511

Moriarty's Restaurant,
1116 Walnut St., Philadelphia
(215) 627-7676

Morley's Pub, 36 E. Main St.,
Norristown
(610) 279-2301

O'Malley's Restaurant & Tavern,
8923 West Chester Pike,
Upper Darby
(610) 789-0220

Quinny's Irish Family Restaurant
& Pub, 51 W. Broad St.,
Bethlehem
(610) 866-2240

The Royal Scot Restaurant
& Pub, 400 Bridge St.,
Phoenixville
(610) 983-3071

Shannon Pub, Exit 52 of
Interstate 80, East Stroudsburg
(717) 424-1951

Valley Stream Inn,
748 Bridgetown Pike,
Holland
(215) 750-1994

Ye Olde Limeport Inn, 1505
Limeport Pike, Limeport
(610) 967-1810

CHINESE

Cherry Street Chinese
Vegetarian Restaurant,
1010 Cherry St., Philadelphia
(215) 923-FOOD

China Place, 4059 William
Penn Hwy., Monroeville
(412) 373-7423

China Place, 5440 Walnut St.,
  Pittsburgh
  (412) 687-7423
China Place, 409 Broad St.,
  Sewickley
  (412) 749-7423
Golden Pond, 1006 Race St.,
  Philadelphia
  (215) 923-0303
Imperial Inn, 146 N. 10th St.,
  Philadelphia
  (215) 627-5588
Joe's Peking Duck House,
  925 Race St., Philadelphia
  (215) 922-3277
Joy Tsin Lau Restaurant,
  1026–28 Race St.,
  Philadelphia
  (215) 592-7227
Noodle Heaven, 224 S. Broad
  St., Philadelphia
  (215) 735-6191
Ocean Garden, 942 Race St.,
  Philadelphia
  (215) 928-0451
Sang Kee Peking Duck House,
  238 N. 9th St., Philadelphia
  (215) 925-7532
Sesame Inn, 19 South, 2975
  Washington Rd., McMurray
  (412) 942-2888
Sesame Inn, 715 Washington Rd.,
  Mount Lebanon
  (412) 341-2555
Sesame Inn, North Hills,
  Pittsburgh
  (412) 366-1838
Sesame Inn, Station Square,
  Pittsburgh
  (412) 281-8282

Southeast Chinese Restaurant,
  1000 Arch St., Philadelphia
  (215) 629-1888
Susanna Foo Chinese Cuisine,
  1512 Walnut St., Philadelphia
  (215) 545-2666
Szechuan China Royal,
  727 Walnut St., Philadelphia
  (215) 627-7111
Tang Yean, 220 N. 10th St.,
  Philadelphia
  (215) 925-3993
Tsui Hang Chun, 911–13 Race
  St., Philadelphia
  (215) 925-8901
Yangming, Haverford Ave. and
  Conestoga Rd., Bryn Mawr
  (610) 527-3200
Yumwok, 400 S. Craig St.,
  Pittsburgh
  (412) 687-7777
Yumwok, 124 Sixth St.,
  Pittsburgh
  (412) 765-2222

EAST INDIAN

India Garden, 328 Atwood St.,
  Pittsburgh
  (412) 682-3000
Kiran Palace Indian Cuisine,
  1358 Columbia Ave.,
  Stone Mill Plaza, Lancaster
  (717) 295-9508
Nav Jiwan International
  Tea Room, Route 272 N.,
  240 N. Reading Rd., Ephrata
  (717) 721-8400
New Delhi Indian Restaurant &
  Sweets, 4004 Chestnut St.,
  Philadelphia
  (215) 386-1941

Passage to India, Quality Inn,
525 S. Front St., Harrisburg
(717) 233-1202
Passage to India, 1320 Walnut
St., Philadelphia
(215) 732-7300
Star of India, 412 S. Craig St.,
Pittsburgh
(412) 681-5700

GREEK

Cafe Theodore, 1100 S.
Columbus Blvd., Riverview
Plaza, Philadelphia
(215) 271-6800
Cafe Zesty, 4382 Main St.,
Philadelphia
(215) 483-6226
Gazebo Room, 2nd and
Locust Sts., Harrisburg
(717) 238-6074
South Street Souvlaki,
509 South St., Philadelphia
(215) 925-3026
Suzi's, 130 Sixth St., Pittsburgh
(412) 261-6443
Suzi's, 1704 Shady Ave.,
Pittsburgh
(412) 422-8066

AFRICAN

Dahlak, 4708 Baltimore Ave.,
Philadelphia
(215) 726-6464
Jamaica, Jamaica, 1430 Fifth Ave.,
Pittsburgh
(412) 281-3726
Marrakesh, 517 S. Leithgow St.,
Philadelphia
(215) 925-5929

MIDDLE EASTERN AND KOSHER

Bachri's Indonesian/Middle
Eastern Restaurant,
3821 Willow Ave., Pittsburgh
(412) 343-2213
Famous 4th Street Delicatessen,
700 S. 4th St., Philadelphia
(215) 922-3274
Gerard's, Route 232, 265 Second
Street Pike, Southampton
(215) 355-6180
Mr. Deli and Mrs. Too,
2023 Linglestown Rd.,
Harrisburg
(717) 545-4261
New York Bagel Bakery,
7555 Haverford Rd.,
Philadelphia
(215) 878-8080
PhilaDeli, 410–12 South St.,
Philadelphia
(215) 923-1986
The Coppermill Harvest,
Park Ridge Hotel, 480 N.
Gulph Rd., King of Prussia
(610) 337-1800
Tira Misu Ristorante, 528 S. 5th
St., Philadelphia
(215) 925-3335

MEXICAN

Cantina Especial, 306 Oliver
Ave., Pittsburgh
(412) 391-2122
Cozumel Restaurante Mexicano,
5507 Walnut St., Pittsburgh
(412) 621-5100
El Rodeo, 4659 Jonestown Rd.,
Harrisburg
(717) 652-5340

El Rodeo, 724 Louck Rd., York
    (717) 845-1341
Hotlicks, 5520 Walnut St.,
    Pittsburgh
    (412) 683-2583
Hotlicks, The Galleria,
    1500 Washington Rd.,
    Pittsburgh
    (412) 341-7427
Margaritaville, 2200 E. Carson
    St., Pittsburgh
    (412) 431-2200

Mexican Post, 104 Chestnut St.,
    Philadelphia
    (215) 923-5233
Tequila Junction, Station
    Square, Pittsburgh
    (412) 261-3265
Zocalo, 36th St. and Lancaster
    Ave., Philadelphia
    (215) 925-5929

APPENDIX C

Ethnic Food Sources, Importers, and Retailers

A. Caravela, 4946 N. 5th St.,
   Philadelphia
   (215) 457-1481
Portuguese foods and ingredients

A. Esposito Meats, 1001 S. 9th
   St., Philadelphia
   (215) 922-2659
*specialty meat products for ethnic
cooking*

Anastasi Seafood,
   905 and 1035 S. 9th St.,
   Philadelphia
   (215) 922-4828
*seafood selections for ethnic
cooking*

Armenian Delight, 2591 West
   Chester Pike at Route 320,
   Broomall
   (610) 353-7711
*Middle Eastern foods and
ingredients*

Assouline & Ting, Inc.,
   314 Brown St., Philadelphia
   (215) 627-3000
*imported gourmet foods, ethnic
ingredients, cooking classes*

Au Fin Palais, 120 Market St.,
   Philadelphia
   (215) 629-9610
assorted French pastries

Avatar's, 321 Bridge St.,
   New Cumberland
   (717) 774-7215
*Middle Eastern foods and
ingredients*

Baker Street, 8009
   Germantown Ave.,
   Philadelphia
   (215) 248-2500 and
   103 Coulter Ave., Ardmore
   (610) 649-8842
European breads

Bird-in-Hand Bakery, 2715 Old
   Philadelphia Pike, Bird-in-
   Hand
   (800) 524-3429
*Pennsylvania Dutch foods,
ingredients, baked goods*

Bitar Specialty Food Market,
   947 Federal St., Philadelphia
   (215) 755-1121
Middle Eastern foods and ingredients

Blumenfield Specialty Foods,
   Great Valley Shopping Center,
   North Versailles
   (412) 829-3004
*Middle Eastern foods, ethnic
ingredients*

Cake and Kandy Emporium,
Village Common, 2019
Miller Rd., East Petersburg
(800) 577-5728
Pennsylvania Dutch sweets

Charcuterie Française,
30th Street Station,
2951 Market St., Philadelphia
(215) 222-3299
French meats

The Cheese Alley, 129 N.
Wayne Ave., Wayne
(610) 688-0819
imported cheeses

Chef's Market, 231 South St.,
Philadelphia
(215) 925-8360
ethnic ingredients, imported foods

Chestnut Hill Cheese Shop,
8509 Germantown Ave.,
Chestnut Hill
(215) 242-2211
imported cheeses

Chung May Food Market,
1017–21 Race St.,
Philadelphia
(215) 625-8883
*Chinese foods, imported
ingredients*

Claudio, King of Cheese,
924–26 S. 9th St.,
Philadelphia
(215) 627-1873
Italian imports, cheeses

Coté & Company, Cross Keys
Plaza, 800 N. Easton Rd.,
Doylestown
(215) 340-2683
imported foods, ethnic ingredients

Cronin's Irish Cottage, 1326 N.
Keyser Ave., Scranton
(717) 342-4448
Irish imports, gourmet foods

Crossroads Bake Shop, Cross
Keys Plaza, 812 N. Easton
Rd., Doylestown
(215) 348-0828
European breads

Dae Han Oriental Food Store,
326 Atwood St., Pittsburgh
(412) 682-2111
Oriental foods and ingredients

Di Bruno Brothers, 930 S. 9th St.,
Philadelphia
(215) 922-2876
Italian ingredients, imported foods

Donatelli's Italian Food Center,
4711 Liberty Ave., Pittsburgh
(412) 682-1406
Italian foods and ingredients

Donegal Square, 523 Main St.,
Bethlehem
(610) 866-3244 and
31 S. State St., Newtown
(215) 504-0626
Irish foods, imported ingredients

Ethnic Foods, 4372 Murray Ave.,
Greenfield
(412) 421-6708
ethnic ingredients, imported foods

Fiorella Brothers, 817 Christian
St., Philadelphia
(215) 922-0506
Italian sausages

F. J. Donovan's, 8117 Old York
Rd., Elkins
(215) 576-1274
Irish food, catering

Fresh Fields, 821 W. Lancaster
Ave., Wayne
(610) 688-9400 and
Gwynedd Crossing Shopping
Center, 1210 Bethlehem
Pike, North Wales
(215) 646-6300
*imported organic foods, ethnic
ingredients*

Gateway Cheese & Coffee,
Gateway Shopping Center,
231 Swedesford Rd., Wayne
(610) 687-5420
imported cheeses, coffee, food gifts

Gerard's, Route 232, 265 Second
Street Pike, Southampton
(215) 355-6180
*Jewish deli ingredients, imported
foods*

G.G.P. Oriental Super Market,
545 S. Broad St., Lansdale
(215) 885-2188
*Korean, Chinese, Japanese
ingredients*

Gigante's Groceria,
1268 Brinton Rd., Pittsburgh
(412) 242-0256
Italian foods and ingredients

Guarrera's Quality Meats,
8th and Catherine Sts.,
Philadelphia
(215) 922-0736
*specialty meats for many ethnic
recipes*

Hesh's Eclair Bake Shop,
7721 Castor Ave., Philadelphia
(215) 728-9331
Jewish baked goods

House of Tea, Ltd., 720 S. 4th St.,
Philadelphia
(215) 923-8327
imported teas

India Grocers, 2101 Greentree
Rd., Scott
(412) 429-5362
East Indian foods and ingredients

International Deli, 1139
Bustleton Pike, Feasterville
(215) 364-2722
*imported foods, ethnic ingredients,
Russian and Ukrainian specialties*

International Food Market,
8570-B Bustleton Ave. at
Placid, Philadelphia
(215) 742-1122
*imported foods, ethnic ingredients,
Russian and Ukrainian specialties*

International Store, 4203 Walnut
St., Philadelphia
(215) 222-4480
East Indian ingredients

Isgro Pastries, 1009 Christian St.,
Philadelphia
(215) 923-3092
Italian sweets, baked goods

Kapoors Indian Imports,
319 S. Craig St., Oakland
(412) 621-1800
*East Indian foods, imported
ingredients*

The Kitchen Shoppe,
101 Shady Lane, Carlisle
(717) 243-0906
*ethnic ingredients, imported foods,
cooking classes*

Ko Ba Woo, 1925 W.
Cheltenham Ave., Elkins Park
(215) 572-1616
Korean ingredients

Kosher Mart, 1916 Murray Ave.,
Pittsburgh
(412) 421-4450
Kosher foods and ingredients

Lee's Produce Market,
1711 Butler Pike,
Conshohocken
(610) 825-4828
*produce for Asian, Mexican, and
Italian cooking*

L. Sarcone & Son Bakery,
756–58 S. 9th St., Philadelphia
(215) 922-0445
Italian breads, pizza

McElroy Imports, 780 Garret Rd.,
Upper Darby
(610) 352-2340
Imported Irish foods

McGinnis Sisters Special
Food Stores, 3825 Saw Mill
Run Blvd., Pittsburgh
(412) 882-6400
ethnic ingredients, imported foods

Metropolitan Bakery, 262 S. 19th
St., Philadelphia
(215) 545-6655 and
1114 Pine St., Philadelphia
(215) 627-3433
European breads

Michael Anastasio Produce, Inc.,
911 Christian St.,
Philadelphia
(215) 627-2807
exotic produce for ethnic recipes

New York Bagel Bakery,
7555 Haverford Rd.,
Philadelphia
(215) 878-8080
authentic bagels, unique spreads

Old City Coffee, Inc., 219–21
Church St., Philadelphia
(215) 629-9292 and
Reading Terminal Market,
1136 Arch St., Philadelphia
(215) 592-1897
*specialty coffees, espresso,
equipment*

Oxford Hall, 311 Bridge St.,
New Cumberland
(717) 774-8789
Irish foods and imports

Pennsylvania Dutch Candies,
408 N. Baltimore Ave., Mt.
Holly Springs
(717) 486-3496
Pennsylvania Dutch confections

The Produce Center, 2305 Darby
Rd., Havertown
(610) 789-6320
*Middle Eastern foods and
ingredients*

Rieker's Prime Meats,
7979 Oxford Ave.,
Philadelphia
(215) 745-3114
*German meats and other German
food specialties*

Ryan's Produce, 1125 Bethlehem
Pike, Ambler
(215) 646-7820
Italian foods, ingredients

Salumeria, Reading Terminal
Market, 12th and Arch Sts.,
Philadelphia
(215) 592-8150 and
2951 Market St., Philadelphia
(215) 222-7444
Italian cheeses, other deli items

Sandy's Scottish Store,
Route 413, Pineville
(215) 598-3523
Scottish foods and imports

S. Clyde Weaver, Lancaster
County Farmers' Market,
Lancaster Ave. and Eagle Rd.,
Wayne-Strafford
(610) 688-9856
imported cheeses

Shammo's Quality Foods
4610 Trindle Rd.,
Camp Hill
(717) 761-5570
imported foods, ethnic ingredients

Siegfried's German Gourmet
Store, Reading Terminal
Market, 12th and Filbert Sts.,
Philadelphia
(215) 922-7029
German foods

The Spice Corner, 949 S. 9th
St., Philadelphia
(215) 925-1660
ethnic spices

Stagno's Italian Accent,
1747 Chislett St., Pittsburgh
(412) 361-2093
*Italian foods and specialty
ingredients*

Talluto's Authentic Italian Food,
944 S. 9th St., Philadelphia
(215) 627-4967
Italian ingredients

Tokyo Japanese Food Store,
5853 Ellsworth Ave.,
Pittsburgh
(412) 661-3777
Japanese foods and ingredients

12th Street Cantina, Reading
Terminal Market, 12th and
Arch Sts., Philadelphia
(215) 625-0321
*Mexican foods and specialty
ingredients*

Villanova Cheese, Inc., 1776 E.
Lancaster Ave., Paoli
(610) 647-8567
imported cheeses

Walnut Acres, Penns Creek
(800) 433-3998
*imported organic foods, ethnic
ingredients*

Yang's Farmers' Market,
573 Lancaster Ave., Berwyn
(610) 644-6635
*specialty ethnic ingredients,
including Asian, Italian, and
Middle Eastern*

Young's Oriental Grocery Store,
5813 Forward Ave.,
Pittsburgh
(412) 422-0559
Oriental foods and ingredients

Zingaro's Italian Store,
439 Railroad, Bridgeville
(412) 221-2088
Italian food specialties

Index